Hemi Muscle

First published in 2006 by Motorbooks, an imprint of MBI Publishing Company, Galtier Plaza, Suite 200, 380 Jackson Street, St. Paul, MN 55101-3885 USA

MBI Publishing Company titles are also availableat discounts in bulk quantity for industrial or sales-promotional use. For details write to Special Sales Manager at MBI Publishing Company, Galtier Plaza, Suite 200, 380 Jackson Street, St. Paul, MN 55101-3885 USA

Library of Congress Cataloging-in-Publication Data

Genat, Robert, 1945-
    Hemi muscle / Robert Genat.
        p. cm.
    Includes index.
    ISBN-13: 978-0-7603-2678-7 (softbound)
    ISBN-10: 0-7603-2678-9 (softbound)
    1. Chrysler automobile—History. 2. Muscle cars—History. 3. Chrysler automobile—Motors—History. I. Title.
    TL215.C55G448 2006
    629.222--dc22
                                        2006017042

Editor: Peter Schletty
Designer: Liz Tufte

Printed in China

On the cover: Hockey Stick stripes were optional for the 1970 'Cuda with an engine callout added to the end. These stripes were only available in black.

On the frontispiece: When equipped with a Hemi engine, Dodge designers placed this small HEMI emblem on the 1968 Charger's door.

On the title pages: Dodge fitted all of its 1970 Hemi Challenger R/T models with Rallye wheels and white letter Goodyear tires.

On the back cover, left: When introduced in 2005, the new Dodge Magnum offered the same new Hemi engine as the Chrysler 300 along with the versatility of a station wagon. **Middle:** In the mid-1960s, the Chrysler Hemi was the preferred power plant for top fuel dragsters. The headers on this dragster are called "weed burners" for obvious reasons. **Right:** For the 1970 Hemi Road Runner, Plymouth carried over the original body it released in 1968 for a third and final year.

About the Author

Robert Genat is a veteran automotive author of such titles as *Mopar Muscle*, *Hemi: The Ultimate American V-8*, and *The Birth of Hot Rodding*. He and his wife, Robin, own and operate ZoneFivePhoto in Encinitas, California.

Contents

Introduction

Hemi Muscle Gallery

The name Hemi has become synonymous with maximum V-8 engine performance. It was not the first overhead-valve V-8 engine to go into production, but it had the most potential for horsepower. In its first generation in the 1950s, the Hemi engine was not used to its fullest potential. But when brought back in 1964, the Hemi, now boasting a hearty 426 cubic inches, proved its true mettle as a race engine. This second-generation Hemi engine quickly set records and embarrassed the competitors who badgered the rule makers to level the playing field. Chrysler's street Hemi engines set the high-water mark for the burgeoning muscle car era. As the muscle car era died, so did the Hemi engine. When production ended at the end of 1971, few tears were shed, since the insurance industry had already sucked most of the oxygen out of the muscle car movement. And with new emissions rules on the horizon, Chrysler pulled the plug on its 426 Hemi engine. As everything from bell-bottom pants to sideburns have made a

comeback, so, too, has the Hemi engine. Initially designed as a replacement engine for Chrysler's 360-ci truck engine, the new 5.7-liter Hemi proved to be a superb engine that was durable and capable of excellent horsepower. It quickly fulfilled the performance legacy of the Hemi engines that had preceded it. Chrysler wasted no time fitting it into its new LX platform cars. Then, without missing a beat, the company created the modern muscle car by offering steroid-pumped SRT8 versions of the Chrysler 300C, Dodge Magnum, and Dodge Charger.

Overhead-valve automotive engines first appeared in 1949. That year both Cadillac and Oldsmobile offered high-compression engines that were revolutionary. Chrysler was not in good shape in 1949, only offering antiquated flathead, inline engines for its passenger cars. Chrysler's engineers used what they had learned while building aircraft engines during World War II to develop their new V-8. This new V-8 would have the most efficient combustion chamber design—a Hemi.

Chrysler introduced its first Hemi engine in 1951. Chrysler's new Fire Power V-8 developed 180 horsepower and was only available in its New Yorker, Imperial, and Saratoga models. Chrysler's Hemi engine was so named because of its hemispherical combustion chamber. This combustion chamber design is exceptionally efficient because of its minimal surface area and valve placement. Chrysler augmented this superb design with the addition of exceptionally well-designed intake and exhaust manifolds.

In 1952 Chrysler's DeSoto division got its first Hemi Firedome engine and, in 1953, Dodge followed with its Red Ram V-8. Each of these engines was similar in design to the Chrysler Fire Power V-8, but displacements and horsepower ratings differed and most components were not interchangeable.

By 1953, Americans were ordering more V-8s than six-cylinder engines in their new cars. The expansion of the nation's highway system fostered this appetite for more powerful V-8s.

It's Saturday night on Detroit's fabled Woodward Avenue, and a Hemi 'Cuda and a Hemi 1969 Road Runner have stopped to fill up with premium.

In 1956, the federal government approved the Highway Act, which called for a 41,000-mile interstate highway system creating a nationwide network of highways. The road was now literally paved for bigger and more powerful cars.

Chrysler's Hemi-design engines led the pack in their capacity to develop horsepower. As gasoline octane ratings rose, Chrysler engineers increased the compression ratios of their engines to take advantage of the horsepower gains available from better fuel. They also increased cam timing and added dual four-barrel intake manifolds. In 1955, Chrysler's 331-ci Fire Power engine developed 300 horsepower. And by 1958, with displacement increased to 392 cubic inches, the Chrysler Fire Power V-8 developed 390 horsepower.

While Chrysler's engineers worked under the hood, its excellent team of designers led by Virgil Exner, was creating some of the most dynamic designs of the era. With the 1955 C-300, Chrysler created a reversal of trends by eliminating the abundance of chrome applied to the exterior. This groundbreaking car also featured a special heavy-duty suspension that lowered the car by 1 inch and included optional chrome-wire wheels. The culmination of 1950s design excellence had to be the 1957 Chrysler 300C. Simply parked at the curb, it looked like the latest air force jet fighter waiting for takeoff.

Hot rodders have always been the earliest to adopt automotive technology. Not long after Ford released its first V-8, young enthusiasts had adapted dual-carburetor intake manifolds and high-compression heads for more power. As

Burn-outs can be made with the flick of the throttle in a 1970 Hemi 'Cuda.

soon as the new overhead-valve engines were released in the late 1940s, the nation's hot rodders sat up and took notice. While these new engines were heavier than the trusty flathead, their potential for horsepower was much higher. By the late 1950s, the Hemi engine would be developing as much as 1,000 horsepower in dragsters. Today, the Hemi engine design is the only one used in Top Fuel dragsters and Funny Cars, where horsepower is estimated as high as 8,000 and speeds are in excess of 330 miles per hour.

The production of Chrysler's first-generation Hemi engine ended in 1958. Dodge and DeSoto ended Hemi production a year earlier. Chrysler's engineers had developed a new series of wedge-combustion engines that developed adequate power and were less expensive to build. The bottom line was that the Hemi engine offered more horsepower (and horsepower potential) than what their average customer actually needed–so, goodbye Hemi.

In the 1950s, America was car crazy–any activity that involved a car flourished, including drive-in restaurants, drive-in movies, and especially auto racing. The

National Association for Stock Car Auto Racing (NASCAR) was formed in 1948 to promote the racing of "stock" cars. While the initial concept included cars that were identical to those that could be bought new in a car dealership, this changed by 1960 to purpose-built race cars that only looked like production cars. The tracks were also getting longer and reached a high point in 1959 with the construction of the 2½-mile Daytona International Speedway.

Chrysler's new generation of wedge combustion engines was powerful, but not powerful enough to be consistent winners in these races. Chrysler engineers were given the mandate to win the 1964 Daytona 500, NASCAR's premier event. To do so they resurrected the Hemi engine design. This new, second-generation Hemi would displace 426 cubic inches. While the new Hemi looked like the previous Hemi engines, it was completely new, and like previous Hemi engines, had an amazing potential for horsepower.

In 1970, Chrysler introduced its first pony cars–the Plymouth Barracuda and Dodge Challenger. While late to the market, they were more exciting than Chevrolet's Camaro or Ford's Mustang. They also offered the Hemi engine. But the muscle car glory days would only last until 1971, as insurance companies added surcharges to muscle cars that made a monthly insurance premium higher than a car payment. With new emissions regulations on the horizon, Chrysler decided it best to pull the plug on the 426 Hemi engine.

Whenever anything is popular, copies start to appear. In the world of automobiles, small-block Corvettes were turned into big blocks, and standard Pontiac Le Mans coupes were turned into GTOs. Commonly called "clones," some of these Corvettes and GTOs were unfortunately passed off as originals. Today, "recreation" is the politically correct term for a clone car. They no longer have the stigma of a rip off, primarily because buyers are more sophisticated. Because of the limited number of Hemi cars originally built, it was inevitable that Hemi clone cars would be built. The first were reproductions of the Super Stock race cars from 1964 and 1965. Then came the B- and E-body cars of the 1960s and 1970s. Now it's possible to have the look and performance of an original Hemi car at half the price.

Almost three decades would pass before Chrysler introduced its third-generation Hemi engine. This time it was not unleashed to win races, but to replace an aging wedge engine in its line of Dodge trucks. Chrysler's engineers did not start with a Hemi engine in mind, but after investigating many designs, decided that a 5.7-liter Hemi would be the best overall engine design to meet their requirements.

When Chrysler's product planners sat down to outline Chrysler's replacement for its LH front-wheel-drive platform, the new Hemi engine was not part of the equation. They knew only that they needed a new car and that a rear-wheel-drive platform would give them the design proportions required. Chrysler called its new platform LX, and it would first include two models: the Dodge Magnum station wagon and the upscale Chrysler 300C. The stylish Charger would be included a year later. Chrysler's timing was perfect, combining the new rear-wheel-drive platform with the new Hemi engine.

Chrysler's SRT (Street and Racing Technology) group could not wait to develop an SRT8 package for these new LX cars. In doing so they increased the displacement to 6.1 liters and upped the horsepower to 425. Zero-to-60 times are in the 5-second range, and any one of the SRT8 cars can run the quarter-mile in 14 seconds. In addition, the SRT engineers added bigger brakes and an aggressive set of 20-inch wheels with wide sticky rubber.

Hemi has come to define many different aspects of automotive history. It was one of the first production V-8s in the 1950s. It was re-introduced in the 1960s to win NASCAR races on the track and be a muscle car on the street. Today, it has been reintroduced in its most refined format—the modern American muscle car reborn with a Hemi.

The Hemi engine makes so much power because of the hemispherical combustion chamber and large valves.

Chapter 1

1950s Hemi Cars

The 1950s were a time of unprecedented growth in America. The economy was humming along, driven by new products and a bright outlook on the future. The government saw the need for the expansion of the nation's network of highways and was investing millions of dollars in this important infrastructure. At the same time, the automobile manufacturers were developing exciting new models with powerful engines to take advantage of these wide-open superhighways.

Chrysler built this cutaway of a Hemi engine to impress auto show attendees with its engineering excellence. *PhotoCourtesy of DaimlerChrysler Archives*

Chrysler's engineers took the knowledge they had gained building aircraft engines during World War II and applied it to automobile engine design. Henry Ford set the trend for future automobile engines with the V-8 engine he designed in 1932. The 90-degree V-8 engine was more powerful and small enough to replace any six-cylinder or straight-eight engine. Automobile customers in the 1950s were traditionally brand loyal and took every opportunity to extol the virtues of their particular brand of car. Each brand in the 1950s had its own unique V-8 engine design and that was used as a selling point. Using its aircraft design experience from the war years, Chrysler chose a design that included a hemispherical combustion chamber. This design is exceptionally efficient but costly to engineer and manufacture because of its complexity.

Chrysler's first passenger car V-8 with the hemispherical combustion chamber was the 331-ci V-8 engine that was installed in the 1951 Chrysler. Called Fire Power, this engine developed 180 horsepower. While adequate by 1951 standards, this engine had the potential to make much more horsepower. By 1955, this engine would be producing 300 horsepower. Chrysler took advantage of the engine's capacity to breathe efficiently and added a dual four-barrel intake manifold. Engineers also increased the compression by one point and modified the cam timing.

In 1952, De Soto got its first V-8, and in 1953 Dodge followed suit. These engines also used the hemispherical combustion chamber design, but were not interchangeable with Chrysler's V-8 or with each other. In 1956, both the Dodge and De Soto V-8s were given the dual four-barrel intake manifolds to take advantage of the Hemi's breathing capacity. But 1957 would be the last year for the Hemi engine design in these two models. The De Soto engine was now developing 345 horsepower and the Dodge, 325 horsepower—as much or more horsepower than any other V-8s on the market.

The only exception to the horsepower levels of the De Soto or Dodge was parent manufacturer Chrysler. In 1957, its Hemi engine had grown to 392 cubic inches and, depending on compression ratio, developed 375 or 390 horsepower. These two exceptionally powerful engines could only be ordered in the 300C model. In 1958, the last year for the Hemi, the 300D offered the 392 Hemi with either 380 or 390 horsepower. These would be the most powerful of the first-generation production Hemi engines and also the last. In 1959, the Hemi engine was only a memory, as Chrysler designated a new generation of wedge-engine designs as their corporate engines.

As the decade of the 1950s came to a close, America's appetite for cars was as big as ever. To remain competitive, Chrysler had to economize and was the first of the major automobile manufactures to realize that a corporate V-8 made good business sense. These new engines, with wedge-combustion chambers, were powerful and less costly to build than the Hemi. While not having the same underhood elegance as the Hemi, they functioned perfectly in the role in which they were cast—a low-cost, powerful V-8.

Chrysler's 300 series of cars offered unmatched elegance with Hemi performance. The 1957 300C also gave the world these stylish tail fins.

Chrysler trimmed the interior of each 1955 C-300 in luxurious tan leather. *David Newhardt*

Chrysler used the modestly finned taillight of the Windsor on the C-300. *David Newhardt*

Below: Chrysler's engineers created a special suspension package for the 1955 C-300 that lowered the car by one inch. *Photo Courtesy of DaimlerChrysler Archives*

David Newhardt

To create the elegant 1955 C-300, Chrysler's designers fused the two-door, hardtop body of the Windsor with the front clip from an Imperial. The stark simplicity of the C-300 contrasted sharply with the kitschy look of other Chrysler models. The application of a single chrome side spear reflected the designer's desire for less chrome. A subtle "300" in slanting chrome letters was placed at the end of each spear. The clean-shaven hood of the C-300 enhanced its simple lines. A special 300 emblem on a black-and-white checkerboard background nestled on the V-shaped panel between the egg-crate grille. Above this, simple chrome letters spelled out the name "Chrysler." Designers also placed the same checkerboard emblem on the deck lid and repeated the use of the checkerboard theme on the center of the 300's standard full wheel covers. Wire wheels were optional.

C-300 Specs
Base price: $4,110
Production: 1,725
Wheelbase: 125.0 inches
Overall length: 218.6 inches
Horsepower: 300 @ 5200 rpm
Torque: 342 ft-lbs @ 3200 rpm

Photo Courtesy of DaimlerChrysler Archives

In addition to the high-performance C-300, Chrysler produced several other models in 1955, with the Fire Power Hemi engine. The all-new 1955 Chryslers were designed by Virgil Exner and called the "100 Million Dollar Look" because of the amount of money Chrysler invested in this completely redesigned series of cars. This would also be the first year Chrysler offered only V-8 engines. The Windsor was Chrysler's entry-level model with two two-door hardtops, a convertible, a station wagon, and a four-door sedan. The next step up was the classy New Yorker. There were two hardtops, the Newport and the upgraded St. Regis. In addition, the New Yorker models were also available in convertible, four-door sedan, and station wagon body styles. Unique bodyside moldings and front and rear bumper treatments differentiated the Windsor from the New Yorker. Chrysler's sales for 1955 boosted it to number two in the luxury car category behind Cadillac.

1955 Chrysler Prices

Windsor Nassau two-door hardtop: $2,703

Windsor Newport two-door hardtop: $2,818

Windsor convertible: $3,090

New Yorker Newport two-door hardtop: $4,140

New Yorker St. Regis two-door hardtop: $3,690

New Yorker convertible: $3,924

The Chrysler C-300's big
Hemi engine was topped
by a "batwing" air cleaner.
*Photo Courtesy of DaimlerChrysler
Archives*

The 1955 Chrysler C-300 set records and put Chrysler on America's racing map.
Photo Courtesy of DaimlerChrysler Archives

In 1956, DeSoto offered two series, the Firedome and Fireflite, both Hemi-powered. DeSoto also offered a limited-production Adventurer two-door hardtop, which was also Hemi powered. It was also in 1956 that DeSoto grew its first set of fins and got rid of its big grille teeth. The fins, albeit tame, were accentuated with a strip of stainless steel that ran the length of the car and abruptly angled up the end of the quarter panel. The taillights went from single, small, vertical, rectangular-shaped lens units to a trio of vertically stacked round lights inset into a notch in the end of the quarter panel. Replacing the teeth was a fine mesh grille with a V emblem in the center. The turn signals were housed in a pair of grille/bumper guards.

1956 DeSoto Prices
Adventurer two-door hardtop: $3,678
Fireflite four-door hardtop: $3,341
Power steering: $97
Power brakes: $40
Power front seat: $70

Above left: Beneath the rear edge of the 1956 DeSoto's tail fin are its vertically stacked taillights.

Above right: In the marketplace, the 1956 DeSoto competed against Oldsmobile and Mercury and had to offer a high level of interior luxury to attract buyers.

Left: DeSoto's 1956 Fireflite 330-ci Hemi developed 255 horsepower.

Following World War II, Chrysler introduced the Imperial as an upgraded Chrysler model. It wasn't until 1954 that Chrysler created the Imperial as a separate brand and allowed it to have its own personality. One of the first things that the Imperial designers did for the 1955 and 1956 models was to add the unique freestanding taillights that have been jokingly referred to as "sparrow strainers." But even the most casual eye could see that the Imperial was based on the Chrysler. All 1956 Imperials were equipped with the 353-ci Hemi. The Imperial series was offered in a two-door hardtop, four-door sedan, and four-door hardtop. The upscale Crown Imperial was only offered in a four-door sedan and limited-edition limousine. These two models were built in limited numbers and cost almost $8,000 each. Production for all 1956 Imperials totaled 10,685 units.

1956 Imperial Fact

By 1956, Chrysler's Imperial was seen as one of the most prestigious luxury cars on the road. Its success is noted by the fact that, in 1956, Chrysler separated the Imperial production numbers from those of the Chrysler car line. In 1956, Chrysler also dedicated two separate production facilities to the Imperial car line. Base prices for 1956 Imperials ranged from $4,832 for a four-door sedan to $7,737 for the 8-passenger stretch limo version.

Left: The 1965 Imperials were trimmed with a combination of brocade cloth and leather.

Right: All 1956 Imperials used the Chrysler Fire Power Hemi engine.

Left: These highly distinctive, freestanding taillights were used on the 1955 as well as the 1956 Imperials.

David Newhardt

A DeSoto Fireflite Pacesetter convertible lead the field of 33 to the green flag at Indianapolis in 1956. DeSoto painted this special model car white and gold, and loaded it with every option that they had (including a record turntable), except air conditioning. The total weight of this car was 4,490 pounds. *Hot Rod* magazine editors had a chance to road-test this car shortly before the race. Powering the car was a 255-horsepower, 330-ci Fireflite Hemi. From a standing start, the big DeSoto could reach 60 miles per hour in 9.8 seconds, an excellent time considering the weight of the car. They also found the car's stopping power to be excellent, because of its 12-inch power-assisted drum brakes. They ran it hard, but the brakes never faded. The editors were disappointed in the lack of feel with power steering, an option required on a car of this weight class. One surprise they noted was the 17.0 miles per gallon it racked up on the highway.

> *Hemi DeSoto Fact*
>
> **In addition to the special Pacesetter convertible, DeSoto also released the limited-edition Adventurer two-door hardtop. This car was often called the "Golden Adventurer" because of its gold-colored trim. DeSoto installed a dual-quad 341-ci Hemi rated at 320 horsepower. One Adventurer paced the 1956 Pikes Peak Hillclimb and another competed in the Daytona Speed Weeks competition.**

Right: The rectangular box below the instrument panel on this 1956 DeSoto Pacesetter is a record player. *David Newhardt*

Left: The DeSoto Fireflite Hemi installed in the 1956 DeSoto pace car developed 255 horsepower. *David Newhardt*

Left: Accentuating the Pacesetter's white and gold paint were gold-colored wheel covers. *David Newhardt*

The Dual Ghia was a custom-built sports car featuring a perfect combination of Italian styling and Chrysler engineering. The Ghia facility in Turin, Italy, crafted the elegant bodies. Once complete, the bodies were shipped to Detroit and mated to the chassis. The Dual Ghia used the rugged, dependable, and well-proven Dodge chassis, Hemi engines, and transmissions. This made for an impressive package, especially since the optional Dodge D-500 Hemi's horsepower ratings were consistently higher than those of the Corvette. This use of humble underpinnings allowed the car to be repaired locally with standard Mopar parts. Production of Dual Ghias began in 1956 and quietly ended in 1958.

Dual Ghia Fact

The A-list of 1950s Dual Ghia owners included popular Hollywood celebrities such as Debbie Reynolds, Lucille Ball, and Frank Sinatra. Each owned one of these cars at one time or another, and so did a few of Sinatra's pals in the famous "Rat Pack." Rat-Packer Peter Lawford even drove one on his television series, *The Thin Man*.

![Dual Ghia engine compartment showing the Dodge Red Ram Hemi engine.]()

Dual Ghias were all equipped with Dodge Red Ram Hemi engines.

The Dual Ghia's machine-turned instrument panel featured a 120-mile-per-hour speedometer and a tachometer.

Chrome-wire wheels accentuated the dramatic styling of the Dual Ghia.

1950s Maximum Factory Hemi Horsepower *

Dodge—The 1957 Dodge Red Ram: 325 cubic inches, 285 horsepower **

DeSoto—The 1957 DeSoto Adventurer: 345 cubic inches, 345 horsepower **

Chrysler—1958 300-D: 392 cubic inches, 380 horsepower **

* These specifications do not include special racing engines or the rare fuel-injected versions.

**Dual-quad carburetion

Above left: This ad for the 1956 DeSoto touts the fact that its 320-horsepower engine is capable of 137 miles per hour.

Above: This ad for the 1956 Dodge D-500 unflinchingly flaunted its horsepower with: "It's a Real Bomb!" And "America's Acceleration Champion."

Left: In 1957, DeSoto proudly announced its 345-horsepower engine could be ordered in its stylish Adventurer.

In the 1950s, the auto manufacturers freely advertised the horsepower ratings of their new cars. There were no restrictions or stigma attached to having a powerful car. Everyone in the 1950s was sure that there was an indefinite supply of oil. This was reaffirmed by the competition for business between gas stations by offering lower prices for gas and giving away sets of steak knives for a fill-up. Other than racing, two other factors drove this need for horsepower: the cars were getting heavier, and the new system of interstates begged for high-speed cruising. So when Chrysler offered dual-quads on its Hemi engines, no one objected. Chrysler freely dotted its advertising with its on-track accomplishments to reconfirm to everyone that they were the horsepower leaders of the American automobile manufacturers.

The 1957 300C had the distinction of being the most powerful car on the road, as well as one of the most beautiful. For 1957, it was available in both a hardtop and a convertible. The 300C's overall lines were clean, from its quad headlights to its tall tail fins. While extra chrome was added to DeSotos and other Chrysler models, the 300C was almost completely free of side trim, except for a thin, quarter-panel molding that ended in a circular red, white, and blue 300C emblem. In addition to the 375-horsepower Hemi engine, one of the highlights of the 1957 300C package was its suspension. Like all 1957 Chrysler passenger cars, the 300C rode on front torsion bars. The standard bars were 1.02 inches in diameter, while the heavy-duty 300Cs were 1.11 inches in diameter. This increased the effective spring rate by 40 percent. The rear springs were semi-elliptical leafs which had a 50 percent increase in spring rate over the standard Chrysler rear springs. The wheels on the 300C were 6.5 inches wide and mounted special Goodyear Blue Streak whitewall tires. At an overall height of 54.7 inches, the 300C had the lowest roofline of all Chrysler products. Chrysler sold 484 300C convertibles and 1,918 hardtops in 1957.

1957 Chrysler 300C
Prices and Specs
Two-door hardtop: $4,929
Convertible: $5,359
Engine displacement:
392 cubic inches
Engine horsepower:
375 @ 5200 rpms
0 to 60 acceleration:
8.0 seconds

Chrysler had to create a pair of low-profile air cleaners because of the 300C's lowered hood profile.

All 1957 Chrysler 300Cs were trimmed in buttery soft leather.

Chrysler added brake cooling scoops below the headlights of the 1957 300C.

Chapter 2

1960s B-Body Hemi Cars

In the late 1950s and early 1960s, the nation's interest in stock car racing encouraged auto manufacturers to build ever more powerful engines so they could share in the prestige of winning these races. Even though in 1957 the Automobile Manufacturer's Association (AMA) adopted a resolution excluding speed and racing from automobile advertising, "Win on Sunday and sell on Monday" became a well-known phrase that meant that a weekend win on the track increased dealership traffic. Everyone wanted to identify with a winner and the public wanted the contact high of having the same model of car that its favorite driver just drove into the winner's circle.

On the surface General Motors abided by the AMA's resolution but still supported racers through a backdoor program. But for both Chrysler and Ford, trying to catch up with General Motors in sales, it was like "knives and chains in a phone booth" for wins on the track.

In 1962, Chrysler's 413-ci wedge engine took on instant hero status among Dodge and Plymouth drag racers with its Max Wedge versions. The popularity of the Max Wedge continued into 1963 with an increase in displacement to 426. While fast on the drag strips, these engines didn't have the legs to win a 500-mile NASCAR race. Chrysler's President Lynn Townsend saw the value in winning races and in April 1963, approached the engineering group with a question: "What will it take to win the 1964 Daytona 500?" Bob Hoover, head of Chrysler's race engine group replied, "If you want to go there and go like stink, let's adapt the Hemi head to the race B engine." In storybook fashion, Richard Petty won the 1964 Daytona 500 driving a 426 Hemi-powered Plymouth hardtop.

This second-generation Hemi engine used the technology of the original, but was adapted to an existing block. Chrysler's engineers used the rocker arm geometry of the original Hemi

When it was released, the 1968 Road Runner rocked the muscle car world.

engines, but tipped the head slightly inboard a few degrees to allow the exhaust pushrod to clear the head gasket bead. This also enhanced the flow line to the intake valve. This new Hemi engine displaced 426 cubic inches, the maximum allowed for NASCAR or NHRA competition. For NASCAR, the 426 Hemi was equipped with a single four-barrel; and for NHRA drag racing, it had two four-barrel carburetors on a cross-ram intake.

The new Hemi's domination of NASCAR led to its ban in 1965. NASCAR required that for an engine to be run on the track, it had to be made available to regular customers. To satisfy this requirement, Chrysler released the street Hemi for the 1966 model year in its Dodge and Plymouth B-body cars. This allowed the Hemi to compete and created one of the greatest muscle car engines of all time.

Chrysler's 1966 Hemi-powered, B-body Coronets and Belvederes were not the best-designed or flashiest cars on the street. Even though they were faster, they didn't have the requisite muscle car stripes or scoops of their mid-1960s counterparts. In 1967 Chrysler corrected the problem by offering the Plymouth

GTX and the Dodge Coronet R/T. While still wrapped in the dated sheet metal, these new models offered stripes, scoops, and redline tires.

For the 1968 model year, Chrysler redesigned its B-body line of cars, offering the customer a vehicle with more contemporary styling. In addition to a beautifully designed Dodge Charger, designers also created the Plymouth Road Runner and the Dodge Super Bee. These new models, along with the return of the GTX and R/T models, provided a wealth of street muscle for Chrysler—especially with the 426 Hemi engine. Plymouth ended the decade on a high note when its 1969 Road Runner was selected as the *Motor Trend* Car of the Year.

Chrysler released the 426 street Hemi in both the Dodge and Plymouth cars to compete in NASCAR races. *Photo Courtesy of DaimlerChrysler Archives*

In 1964 there were no rules from NASCAR dictating that a certain amount of cars needed to be built with a certain engine before that engine could be used in its races. So when Chrysler introduced its 426 Hemi, it only had to maneuver around the slower cars on the track. Shortly after the introduction of the NASCAR 426 Hemi, Chrysler decided it would give the engine to drag racers so they could get in on the fun. The biggest difference between the NASCAR Hemi engine and the Hemi Chrysler built for drag racing was the dual-quad cross-ram intake manifold. Most of the Hemi cars built for drag racing were two-door sedans that were fitted with lightweight body components that went directly to veteran drag racers. But both Dodge and Plymouth also built a limited number of two-door hardtops with the race Hemi engine. These cars could be drag raced, or they could be easily converted by means of a Chrysler-prepared kit, for NASCAR racing.

1964 Hemi Engine Specs
Displacement: 426-ci
Horsepower: 425 @ 6000 rpm
Torque: 480 ft-lbs @ 4600 rpm
Compression ratio: 12.5:1
Carburetion: Dual four-barrels on a cross-ram intake

Above: The Hemi engines sold in Dodge and Plymouth cars in 1964 were fitted with a dual four-barrel cross-ram intake manifold.

Left: A Hurst shifter was added to shift the four-speed transmission backing the Hemi engine.

Below: When Dodge added a Hemi engine to its 440 hardtop, it also added a large hood scoop.

When Chrysler released its street Hemi for 1964, they didn't specify a certain model to create or retain an image. This powerful new engine could be ordered in any of the Coronet intermediate-size models including the four-door sedan and two-door sedan. While most Dodge customers preferred the Coronet 500 two-door hardtop, a few brave souls selected the least expensive two-door sedan because it weighed less than the hardtop. This sacrifice of style for a weight savings was done in the interest of speed. It was simple physics; the less weight an engine has to push, the faster it can push. There was also the sinister side of buying a lowly sedan. On the street it looked like something a senior citizen would drive. This somber look would entice foolish GTO drivers into thinking they could easily win a street race. Within a few seconds of the light changing to green all they saw was the Hemi sedan's taillights.

1966 Coronet
Hemi Production

Two-door sedan: 34

Deluxe two-door sedan: 49

440 two-door hardtop: 288

440 convertible: 21

500 two-door hardtop: 340

500 convertible: 21

With the hood up on this 1966 Coronet sedan, the Hemi's chrome air cleaner gave away the true purpose of this car.

All 1966 street-Hemi-optioned Dodges and Plymouths were fitted with Goodyear Blue Streak tires.

In 1966, Dodge installed an Inland shifter on all of its four-speed equipped street Hemi cars.

Chrysler completely redesigned its B-body Plymouth and Dodge for 1966. While a big improvement over the previous B-body models, they lacked the higher style of the GM products that they were required to compete against. The new B-body Coronets and Belvederes were angular, much like GM's full-size cars of 1962–1964. While attractive, they were at least four years behind the automotive design curve. The restyled 1966 SS396 Chevelles and GTOs featured sexy new bodies with rounded lines. They also offered more street image than the Coronet or Belvedere. The GTO had a hood scoop that could be made functional and the Chevelle's hood had imitation side vents. The GTO offered optional Rallye wheels or Hurst mags with redline tires while the Coronets and Belvederes, with the Hemi, only had blueline tires with full wheel covers. The cars' names were also a problem; Coronet and Belvedere were dated compared to the GTO or SS396. This all would change in 1967.

1966 Plymouth Hemi Production

Belvedere I two-door sedan: 136

Belvedere II two-door hardtop: 531

Belvedere II convertible: 10

Belvedere Satellite two-door hardtop: 503

Belvedere Satellite convertible: 27

The 1966 Belvedere's bench seat interior was simple and functional.

What the new 1966 Belvedere lacked in style it made up for in performance with the street Hemi.

By 1966 automotive styling standards, the Belvedere missed the mark. But it will always be remembered as the first Plymouth to have the optional street Hemi.

1966 Belvedere II convertible Hemi.

It may not have been an ace, but Plymouth did have one card up its sleeve for the 1966 model year—the Belvedere Satellite. The Satellite models were upscale versions of the Belvedere II two-door hardtop and convertible. Plymouth removed the standard Belvedere's side trim and added a thin beltline molding. They also added trim to the wheel openings and rocker panels. A special chrome panel was added to the back of the deck lid between the taillights. The finishing touch was the small red, white, and blue bar next to the Satellite emblem on the deck lid. Plymouth added vinyl covered bucket seats and a console to the interior. A floor shifter was added with the TorqueFlite option. This was Plymouth's first attempt at creating a sporty car and the results were excellent. In 1966 Plymouth sold 35,399 Satellite hardtops and 2,759 convertibles. The 1966 Satellite would be the prototype for the 1967 GTX.

1967 Hemi Satellite Road Test 0 to 60: 5.3 seconds
0 to 100: 12.8 seconds
Quarter-mile: 13.8 seconds at 104 miles per hour
Top speed: 130 miles per hour
Average miles per gallon: 11.0

Above: The 1966 Plymouth Satellite featured standard bucket seats and a stylish console.

Right: Plymouth designers placed a small Satellite emblem along with a red, white, and blue bar on the right side of the deck lid.

Below: Added to the deck lid of the 1966 Plymouth Satellite was a full-width chrome panel.

Plymouth's product planners had their ears to the street and saw that while their Hemi cars were faster than the other cars on the street, they didn't have the strong identity of the GTO, SS396 Chevelle, or Fairlane GT. They knew—with a heritage of building cars for librarians and taxicabs—they had to do something to improve the street cred of Plymouth's top muscle car. Starting with the Satellite, they added a new name, GTX. To upgrade the exterior, Plymouth's designers added a pair of nonfunctional hood scoops along with a set of chrome Road Wheels mounting redline tires. Racing stripes were added that ran across the hood and deck lid (these stripes could be deleted). The highlight of the new GTX was the standard 375-horsepower 440-ci engine. Plymouth only offered one optional engine—the Hemi. This outstanding package sold well and finally put Plymouth on America's muscle car map.

GTX Fact

The GTX handle came about because Jack Smith, Plymouth's chief product planning manager, wanted something that "sounded like GTO." Catchy names were part of the automotive marketing game in the mid-1960s, where a high-horsepower sedan could be turned into a highly identifiable muscle car with the addition of the right name or sequence of letters.

A racing-style gas cap and chrome exhaust tips were added to the GTX.

Each 1967 Plymouth GTX had a 6000-rpm tachometer mounted on the console and a 150-mile-per-hour speedometer.

Plymouth added two of these low-profile hood scoops to the 1967 GTX.

Dodge's B-body model for 1967 was the Coronet and the performance equal of Plymouth's GTX was the R/T (Road and Track) version. To make the R/T stand out, Dodge designers added three large nonfunctional louvers in the center of the R/T's hood and added a unique grille with thin vertical bars. This grille looked similar to the one on the Dodge Charger, but didn't have the Charger's hidden headlights. Redline 7.75x14 tires were standard, but the chrome Road Wheels were optional. Dodge did offer a rocker panel stripe for the R/T, but only a limited number of cars were built with it. This particular Dodge R/T is one of two convertibles built with the Hemi engine in 1967. Most muscle car buyers in the mid-1960s shied away from convertibles as being too expensive, and the additional weight of the convertible body style was a handicap for street racing.

1967 Dodge Coronet R/T Facts

Two-door Hardtop
Production: 9,553
Base price: $3,199
Shipping weight—3,565

Convertible
Production: 628
Base price: $3,438
Shipping weight: 3,640

Left: Vinyl bucket seats were a standard feature of the 1967 Dodge R/T.

Right: All 1967 R/Ts with the Hemi engine were fitted with this chrome air cleaner.

Below: For the 1967 R/T, Dodge designers created a special rear trim panel that echoed the design of the grille.

David Newhardt

In 1968, with one giant step forward, Chrysler made a major advancement in the muscle car wars. The release of the new Road Runner was the shot in the arm Plymouth needed. The 1967 GTX was a fine performance car, but never broke completely away from Plymouth's heritage of low-cost sedans. For 1968, Plymouth decided to strip their newly restyled midsize entry of any frills, add a performance-engine package, and a whimsical cartoon name—Road Runner. With the Road Runner, Plymouth had a low-priced factory hot rod that was capable of kicking any GTO's butt at any stoplight. Plymouth initially introduced the Road Runner as a pillared coupe. A two-door hardtop would be introduced later in the model year, but no convertible. The 1968 Road Runner used the same hood, with side-facing nonfunctional vents, as the GTX. Near the front edge of the doors was a small chrome plate discretely announcing that this was a Road Runner. To the rear of this Road Runner emblem, was a small decal of the crafty little bird at warp speed. Plymouth included a 335-horsepower 383-ci engine as the standard powerplant for the Road Runner with only one optional engine—the Hemi.

> **1968 Hemi Road Runner Fact**
>
> While Plymouth's marketing staff was optimistic about the new 1968 Road Runner, they were also cautious about their sales forecast. They estimated that first year sales would only be 2,500. Plymouth actually sold 44,599 1968 Road Runners. And 1,019 were equipped with a Hemi.

Above: Plymouth only offered one optional engine for the 1968 Road Runner—the 425-horsepower Hemi. *David Newhardt*

Left: In 1968, the cartoon Road Runner decals were black and white. In all other years they were full cartoon color. *David Newhardt*

Right: When a Hemi engine was added to a 1968 Road Runner, Plymouth fitted the car with 15-inch redline tires. *David Newhardt*

Plymouth's other performance car for 1968 was the GTX. With the Road Runner as the low-priced street racer, Plymouth positioned the GTX as the upscale muscle car available as either a two-door hardtop or convertible. The GTX also came with bucket seats, an optional center console, and lots of imitation woodgrain trim. The exterior featured extra chrome trim along the rocker panel and around the wheel openings. A few inches above the rocker panel were two horizontal body stripes that terminated with a large GTX chrome emblem just in front of the rear wheel opening. The GTX's hood featured twin side-facing vents that had the engine size inset in small chrome letters. As in 1967, the GTX came standard with a 375-horsepower 440-ci V-8, but for 1968 Plymouth added the Hemi as an option and 446 people were willing to pay the extra $604.75 for the Hemi.

1968 Plymouth GTX Prices
Two-door hardtop: $3,355
Convertible: $3,590
Hemi engine: $604.75
Sure-Grip rear axle: $42.35
Console: $52.85
Tachometer: $48.70

Left: The 1968 GTX option included comfortable bucket seats and wood-trimmed instrument panel and doors.

Right: The nonfunctional hood vents on the 1968 GTX and Road Runner were used to denote engine size.

Left: The only way to get a Plymouth Hemi convertible in 1968 was to buy a GTX.

In 1969, the Road Runner returned with a vengeance. Sales at 80,000 were almost double the 1968 total. Plymouth's designers only made minor changes to the 1969's grille and taillights. The Road Runner was still the low-priced performance king, but the price was increasing and the option list got longer. A convertible Road Runner was added to the coupe and hardtop models. Power windows, center console, and bucket seats were new to the option list. Standard on any Hemi and optional for the 383, was a Fresh Air hood. This hood was also used on the GTX. It was similar to the hood on the 1968 Road Runner, except the vents were vertical. A system of ductwork extended under the hood that directed fresh air to the engine. While overall sales of the 1969 Road Runner increased, the number opting for the Hemi engine decreased slightly. The hardtops led the list with 422 Hemis, followed by the coupes at 356, and the convertibles at a lowly 10.

1969 Road Runner Prices
Two-door coupe: $2,599
Two-door hardtop: $3,083
Convertible: $3,313
Hemi engine: $813.45
Bucket seats: $100.85
Tachometer: $50.15

Above: The blacked-out panels on the 1969 Road Runner's hood were an option called Performance Hood Paint, an option that cost an additional $18.05.

Left: Plymouth added bucket seats to the Road Runner's option list for 1969.

Below: Motor Trend magazine selected the Road Runner as its Car of the Year in 1969.

HEMI ROAD RUNNER: 0-105 IN 13.5 SECS.! ONE OF THE REASONS MOTOR TREND NAMED IT...

CAR OF THE YEAR

See facts, figures, NHRA acceleration times — Page 127

After *Motor Trend* magazine selected the 1969 Road Runner as its Car of the Year, Plymouth copywriters wanted to give the specific quarter-mile times and speeds that potential buyers wanted to hear. To do so they first established what a showroom-fresh Hemi Road Runner would do. In stock form, a 1969 Hemi Road Runner equipped with a TorqueFlite and 4.10 rear axle consistently ran the quarter-mile in the mid-13-second range at speeds of 105 miles per hour. The next day, the same car was brought back to the track with a few bolt-on performance additions. Plymouth technicians added a Racer Brown cam and kit along with a set of Hooker headers. Run with the headers open, the Hemi Road Runner's elapsed times dropped into the high 12-second range at speeds of 110 miles per hour. Most impressive!

1969 Plymouth Hemi Production

GTX two-door hardtop: 198

GTX convertible: 11

Road Runner coupe: 356

Road Runner two-door hardtop: 422

Road Runner convertible: 10

Left: For the 1969 model year, Plymouth's designers added a full-color, full-speed Road Runner decal to the door.

Right: The intake for the Fresh Air hood was covered with a red screen. Hemi identification was placed on the side of the hood's intake.

Below: Plymouth offered a full-length body stripe for the 1969 Road Runner that ran the length of the car's beltline.

The 1969 Dodge R/T (and Super Bee) received very few changes from their 1968 models. Bumblebee stripes on both models were revised to a single broad stripe. Both the R/T and Super Bee were available with an optional pair of dummy side scoops that were attached to the leading edge of the quarter panel. The Super Bee, previously only available as a two-door coupe, could now be ordered in a hardtop model and bucket seats were an option. The biggest news for both models was the addition of the Ram Charger hood. Standard with the Hemi and optional with other performance engines, the Ram Charger hood fed fresh air to the carburetors. On the surface of the hood, two forward-facing wedge-shaped scoops were attached. Under the hood was a large fiberglass fixture that fed fresh air to the air cleaner. With the Hemi engine, HEMI was spelled out in small chrome letters on the outboard side of each scoop. In 1969, a total of 258 Super Bees and 107 Coronet R/Ts were equipped with the Hemi engine.

1969 Coronet R/T Prices
Two-door hardtop: $3,425
Convertible: $3,643
Hemi engine: $717.90
Quarter-panel scoops: $35.80
Front disc brakes: $50.15

Above: A pair of hood scoops were added as part of the Ram Charger hood that came standard with the Hemi.

Left: Only ten 1969 Dodge Coronet R/T convertibles were optioned with the Hemi engine.

Below: Bumblebee stripes on the 1969 R/T were only available in white, red, or black.

Chapter 3

Chargers & Winged Hemi Cars

When Chrysler completely redesigned its B-body lineup in 1966, it added a new Dodge model—the Charger. Dodge division had always offered slightly more upscale vehicles than Plymouth. While Plymouth fought for sales against Ford and Chevrolet, Dodge saw Mercury and Buick as its competition. The four-passenger personal luxury car market was starting to heat up in the mid-1960s with the Ford Thunderbird and Buick Riviera. It was only natural for Dodge to step up with the Charger for that expanding niche market.

With the 1966 Charger, Dodge pockets were not deep enough to create an entirely new car, so designers built it on the B-body Coronet two-door hardtop platform. To make it stand out, Dodge designers added a striking fastback roofline. They used the massive Coronet R/T grille with added hidden headlights. They fitted the interior with standard bucket seats

and an impressive jet fighter–style instrument panel. And like the other 1966 B-body cars, the 426 Hemi was an available option. Dodge carried over the Charger for the 1967 model year with few changes.

When Chrysler redesigned its B-body line of cars for the 1968 model year, it also redesigned the Charger. Its success in the market allowed Dodge designers to create a completely new design. Still based on the B-body platform, the new Charger was no longer a "made-from" car, but one of the most electrifying new designs to ever come out of the Dodge studios. Its sides had a distinctive Coke-bottle shape that accentuated the wheel openings, and its sleek fastback roofline featured a deeply recessed rear window. This beautiful car had only one flaw—it was not aerodynamic on the high-speed NASCAR tracks. The Charger's deep grille opening acted like a windsock and the recessed rear window disturbed the air flowing over the rear

Dodge's advertising theme for 1966 was the "Dodge Rebellion." Leading the way was the new Charger. *Photo Courtesy of DaimlerChrysler Archives*

deck. In an effort to improve the Charger's aerodynamics, Dodge designers created the Charger 500. These special models had a unique grille that was pulled forward to the edge of the opening and redesigned back glass that smoothed out the roofline.

The Charger 500 was an excellent first step, but Dodge knew there was more speed to be gained by making the car even more aerodynamic. The second step was more drastic and controversial. With the aid of wind tunnel testing, Chrysler engineers created the Dodge Daytona—arguably the most audacious car ever designed. This rare model featured a long pointed nose and a basket-handle-style rear wing. Because of NASCAR's rules requiring race engines also in cars available to the general public, Dodge Daytonas were soon seen on showroom floors and on the streets.

With the on-track success of the Dodge Daytona, Richard Petty, a Plymouth driver, asked when his Daytona would be delivered. When told that as a Plymouth driver he would not be receiving a Dodge, he packed his helmet and signature sunglasses and started driving a Ford. To attract Petty back to the Plymouth camp, the Superbird was created from a 1970 Road Runner. Like the Daytona, the Superbird featured a long pointed nose and a high rear wing. Petty returned to drive a Superbird in 1970, but due to the decline of the muscle car era, many Superbirds went unsold. Today, the Superbird and Dodge Daytona are two of the most highly coveted Mopars, especially those with a Hemi engine.

Plymouth's Superbird was created solely for the purpose of being able to win races in NASCAR. There was nothing practical about the car for everyday driving on the street.

With the personal luxury car class emerging in the mid-1960s, Dodge entered this hot market with its new Charger. Based on the 1966 Coronet, the new Charger offered the buyer a four-place performance car with plenty of unique styling. The most dramatic feature was the sleek fastback roof. Because Dodge did not have the money to create a completely new car, the Charger was a "made from" based on the Coronet. To conceal its Coronet heritage, Dodge designers added an impressive full-width grille with hidden headlights. It was only natural that Dodge add the Hemi engine to the option list. In 1966, 468 Hemi-equipped Chargers rolled off of the assembly line.

Charger Fact

Competing for market share with the Charger in the personal luxury class in 1966 was the Buick Riviera and the Ford Thunderbird. Ford defined this market segment in 1958 when it first offered a four-seat model. Buick came along in 1963 using the same formula to create its Riviera.

Left: The engine compartment on the 1966 Dodge Charger was identical to the one on the Coronet.

Right: Dodge designers created a harmonious look between the front and rear of the 1966 Charger by adding a full-width taillight.

Below: Chrome road wheels were one of the many options a buyer of the new 1966 Charger could select.

1967 DODGE CHARGER HEMI

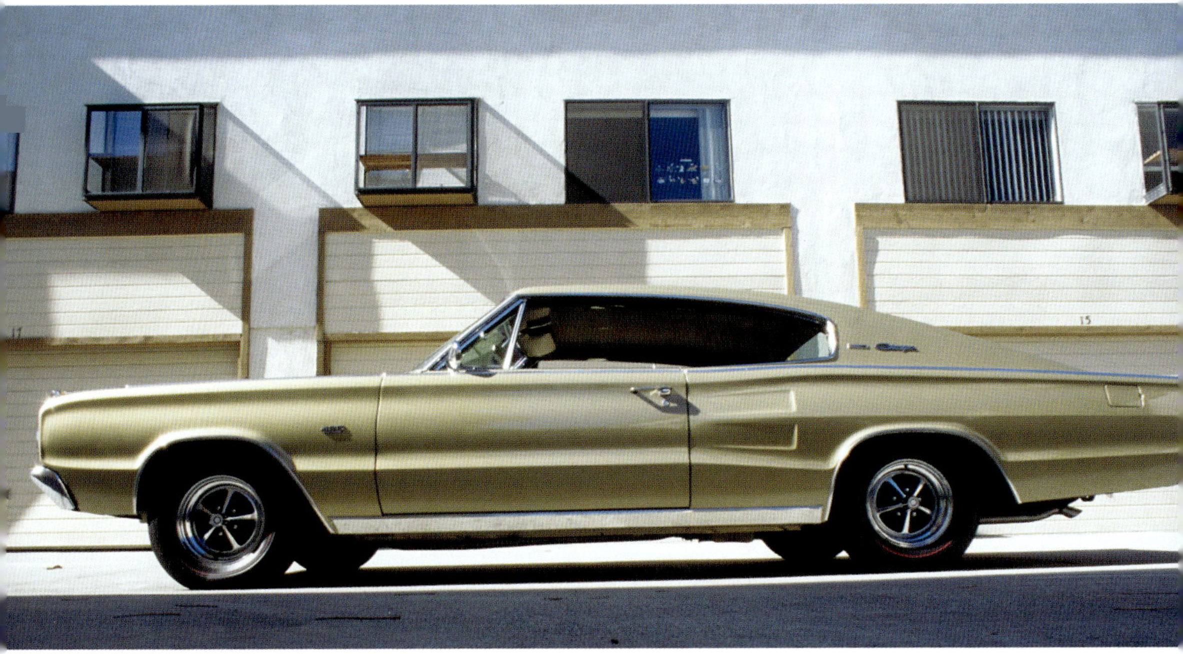

The 1966 Dodge Chargers sold well with 37,334 units rolling out of the showroom doors. Because of its niche market position, it didn't take many sales away from the Coronet, which was a bonus for Dodge. For 1967, Dodge designers left well enough alone and only made minor changes to the Charger. But sales of the Charger in 1967 dropped to half the amount sold in 1966. The number of Hemi-equipped Chargers dropped as well with only 118 Hemi Chargers sold.

1967 Hemi Charger Specs

Wheelbase: 117.0 inches

Curb weight: 4,390 pounds

Top speed: 130 miles per hour

0 to 60: 6.4 seconds

Quarter-mile: 14.16 seconds @ 96.15 miles per hour

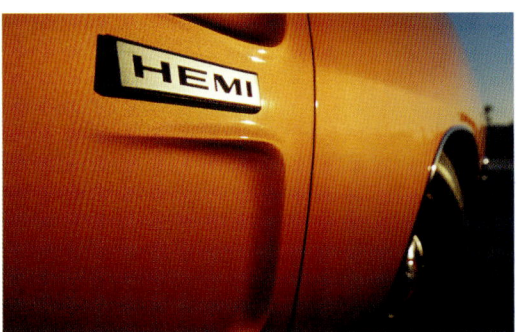

When equipped with a Hemi engine, Dodge designers placed this small HEMI emblem on the door. *David Newhardt*

The only chrome trim Chrysler added to the 1966 Hemi engine was the air cleaner.

Chrysler's excellent integration of the hidden headlight doors on the Dodge Charger makes them almost impossible to detect.

The new Dodge Charger was sheer beauty to the eye of the beholder and looked like it was doing 150 miles per hour while standing still. Unfortunately, at 150 miles per hour and above, it had some serious issues. This classic design had serious aerodynamic drawbacks. In an attempt to fix some of these problems, Dodge designers created the Charger 500. The most noticeable changes were the removal of the tunneled rear window and flush grille. Because of NASCAR's rules, these modified Chargers had to be available to the general public. Dodge scheduled 500 to be built, hence the name "Charger 500." It's generally accepted that only 392 were actually built. Of that number only 67 were built with the Hemi engine.

Charger Fact

The Charger 500's body modifications were done by Creative Industries, a Detroit-area fabrication shop. In the front, they used a Coronet grille and mounted it flush to the front edge of the hood. In the back, they added a new rear window cap eliminating the deeply tunneled rear window. A-pillar covers were added along with two small "500" emblems.

Above: Bumblebee stripes with a "500" cutout were added to the tail of each Charger 500.

Right: For improved aerodynamics, Dodge designers added smooth A-pillar covers to the Charger 500.

Below: The deeply recessed rear window of the new Charger created aerodynamic havoc on the superspeedways. To alleviate this problem, Dodge added a completely new rear window.

Dodge designers added a small center split to the grille of the 1969 Charger and new taillights. Dodge also added the SE (Special Edition) option that could be combined with the R/T option, but it could not be ordered with a Hemi engine. The SE option added leather inserts to the front seats only and other luxury touches. Dodge also added a sunroof to the option list, but the buyers were required to also order a vinyl top. Also added to the option list was a Chrysler sturdy slant-six engine, but most buyers preferred one of the four V-8s. The base V-8 was the 230-horsepower 318. Dodge also offered a 335-horsepower 383, a 375-horsepower 440 (standard on the R/T), and the Hemi.

1969 Charger Dimensions
Overall length: 206.6 inches
Overall width: 76.7 inches
Wheelbase: 117.0 inches
Overall height: 54.2 inches
Shipping weight:
3,671 pounds

In 1969, Dodge sold a total of 432 Hemi-equipped Chargers. This number also includes Hemi installations in Charger Daytonas and Charger 500s.

Charger R/T models were trimmed with red inlayed R/T emblems on the driver's side headlight door.

When a customer ordered a 1969 Charger R/T without the Bumblebee stripes, he received R/T emblems on the quarter panel.

David Newhardt

The aerodynamic changes made to the Charger 500 didn't meet the racing expectations of Dodge executives. They also realized that there was no more horsepower to be extracted from the Hemi so it was back to the aerodynamic drawing board. This time Dodge didn't pull any punches in their quest for aerodynamic and track supremacy. Creative Industries was chosen to build the components and cars for this project. They started where the Charger 500 left off (revised rear window), and in an effort to improve downforce and clean up the front end, an 18-inch pointed extension was added. In the rear, a 23-inch-high wing created downforce for the rear. Small reverse scoops were added to the tops of the front fenders for clearance on the race cars. These scoops were only cosmetics for the street models. Dodge built a total of 500 Daytonas with 700 being Hemi powered.

> **Daytona Fact**
>
> **The entire rear wing on the Daytona was painted one of three colors—red, black, or white—to match the Bumblebee tripe. Cut out of the stripe was the word DAYTONA. This car could not be ordered as a stripe delete.**

The Charger Daytona's nose extension added 18 inches to the length of the car. *David Newhardt*

The scoops on top of the Daytona's front fenders were designed for tire clearance on the Daytona race cars. They were only cosmetic on the street versions. *David Newhardt*

When Richard Petty first saw the new Dodge Daytona, he asked when his was going to be delivered. He was told that as a Plymouth driver, he could not drive a Dodge and therefore would not be getting a Daytona. Unhappy as Chrysler's leading driver, he quit and drove a Ford for the 1969 season. To lure him back, Plymouth created the Superbird. Built by Creative Industries using a 1970 Road Runner as a starting point, the Plymouth Superbird looked similar to the Dodge Daytona, but there were no interchangeable parts. There were a total of 851 Superbirds built.

Superbird Fact

Plymouth's Superbirds were built with three different engines: the 375-horsepower 440, the 390-horsepower Six Barrel 440, and the Hemi. The 375-horsepower 440 engine was not available on the standard 1970 Road Runner. While the Air Grabber scoop was available on the standard Road Runner, it was not available on the Superbird.

Above: All Superbirds were fitted with a vinyl roof. This covered the special rear window cap used to mount the unique rear glass.

Right: The Superbird's rear wing stanchions were decorated with a Road Runner decal. The large "Plymouth" decal on the quarter panel was identical to the one on Petty's Superbird race car.

Below: Plymouth built a total of 135 Superbirds with the Hemi engine.

A change in NASCAR rules required Plymouth to build one Superbird for each dealer. This would have meant building close to 2,000 of the special cars. The production total ended up being 815. With the rising insurance rates for muscle cars and the general public's loss of interest in high-performance cars, many Superbirds sat unsold for as long as a year. Rumors had a few dealers removing the extended nose and high rear wing to take it back to "Road Runner" level just so it could be moved out of the showroom. Much of the Superbird's shine diminished when NASCAR required the racers to run an engine with 305 cubic inches instead of the Hemi. This effectively killed any future aero cars from Chrysler.

Superbird Colors

Alpine White

Vitamin C Orange

Lemon Twist

Lime Light

Blue Fire Metallic

Tor-Red

Corporation (Petty) Blue

The hood of each Superbird had to be extended to match the special nose.

Bucket seats and a center console were available options for the Superbird.

Chapter 4

1970s B-Body Hemi Cars

Chrysler's smartly designed 1968 and 1969 B-body performance models sold well and vaulted Dodge and Plymouth to muscle car superstar status. These exceptionally successful models also gave Chrysler the cash to invest in product design for the next generation of B-body cars, scheduled for release in 1971.

Even without a Hemi engine, the Plymouth Road Runner and Dodge Super Bee were the hottest muscle cars of 1970. These two cars, along with their B-body sisters—GTX and R/T, were given a light facelift to keep pace with styling trends. The Dodge was given a unique front end with a pair of chrome horse collars, while the Plymouth received a tasteful quarter-panel scoop and a cleaner front and rear treatment. In addition to the Hemi, Chrysler also offered the exciting 440 Six Pack engine in its B-body performance cars.

The hottest new designs coming out of Chrysler for 1971 were its new B-body cars.

Plymouth's Road Runner and GTX received a completely new body that was more rounded with an assertive halo grille opening. Dodge dropped its Coronet line and expanded the Charger lineup to include the Super Bee and the Charger R/T. This new Charger also sported an exciting new body, filled with sexy curves.

These new B-bodies featured the latest in automotive design tricks including hidden

The Hurst Pistol Grip shifter has become an icon of Mopar muscle cars.

In 1970, Plymouth added its snarling Air Grabber hood scoop to its Hemi-powered B-body GTX and Road Runner as a standard feature.

of the near epidemic proportions of street racing. Sales of Chrysler's muscle cars saw a significant drop in 1971.

When the last of the 1971 B-bodies rolled off the Chrysler assembly line, an era came to a close. There would be no more 426 Hemi engines and no more multiple carburetion; there would be only V-8s laden with emissions control systems and a few body stripes. The muscle era had ended, but Chrysler left several enormous footprints on its landscape. Many believe that the biggest footprint was the one left by the Hemi engine.

windshield wipers, flush door handles, and ventless, one-piece door glass. But missing from both the 1971 Dodge and Plymouth B-body lineups were convertible models. Convertible sales had been weak in the late 1960s, therefore Chrysler saved the cost of engineering and building these poor selling models for 1971 by simply not offering them. There were also rumblings coming out of Washington about new federal regulations that would require an extensive amount of safety gear for any new convertible design. The new B-body performance models were only available in pillarless two-door coupes.

Chrysler kept its engine lineup intact for 1971. The Hemi engine, along with many of Chrysler's other powerful V-8s could be ordered in any of these models. But the rising cost of auto insurance premiums made many muscle car buyers rethink their purchase options. Also by this time, owning a muscle car had become politically incorrect because

In 1971, Plymouth released its all new highly styled B-body Road Runner and GTX. These two models were only available in two-door coupes—no convertibles.

For 1970, Plymouth carried over the original body it released in 1968 for a third and final year. Plymouth stylists did an excellent job with the light facelift that included a new front and rear treatment. In addition they added a small scoop to the quarter panel. The list of options Plymouth offered gave the customer a wide choice of engine, colors, and unique features. This would also be the last year for the GTX or Road Runner convertibles.

1970 Road Runner Prices

Two-door coupe: $2,896

Two-door hardtop: $3,034

Convertible: $3,289

Hemi engine: $841.05

Bucket seats: $100.85

Above: Plymouth's designers added the whimsical cartoon bird to the center of the steering wheel so the buyer wouldn't forget he was driving the top muscle car of the era.

Above: The 1970 Road Runner's Air Grabber hood scoop included a larger fixture attached to the bottom of the hood that actuated the door and sealed to the base of the air cleaner.

Left: Plymouth placed a small decal of the Road Runner cartoon character on the leading edge of the 1970 Road Runner's front fender.

Like Plymouth did with its 1970 Road Runner and GTX, Dodge also worked a little facelift magic with its Coronet Super Bee and R/T models. Unfortunately, the double horse-collar grille did not resonate with a lot of buyers. This front-end treatment came about because Dodge designers were always a little jealous of Pontiac's split grille and halo style bumper. Even with the controversial front end, the 1970 R/T and Super Bee were still performance bargains. And like the 1970 Road Runner and GTX, this would be the last year for a convertible Coronet R/T (Super Bees were never made as a convertible). This is the only 1970 Coronet R/T convertible built with a Hemi engine.

1970 Dodge R/T Prices
Two-door hardtop: $3,569
Convertible: $3,785
426 Hemi engine: $718.05
Rallye instrument cluster: $90.30
Disc brakes: $27.90

Dodge designers added these slick quarter-panel scoops to the 1970 Coronet R/T.

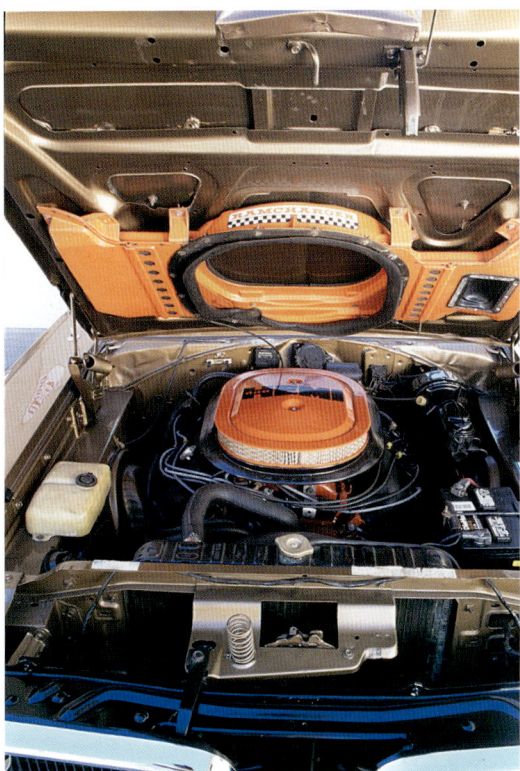

All Hemi-equipped 1970 Coronet R/T and Super Bee models were fitted with a pair of Ramcharger hood scoops. This large orange fixture on the bottom of the hood fed the cool air to the carburetors.

Dodge added these tasteful Hemi emblems to the Ramcharger hood scoops on Hemi-equipped 1970 Coronet Super Bee and R/T models.

Dodge designers did an excellent job in their redesign of the 1971 Charger. They were able to retain the sexiness of the 1968–1970 Charger while adding the latest contemporary design tricks. The new Charger would look equally at home in front of an upscale restaurant as it would street racing on Woodward Avenue. The Charger line completely replaced the aging Coronet two-door models. The two performance models were the R/T and the Super Bee.

1971 Dodge Charger R/T Prices

Two-door hardtop: $3,777

Hemi engine: $746.50

Four-speed transmission: N/C

TorqueFlite transmission: $237.50

AM/FM stereo radio with cassette: $366.40

Power sunroof: $484.65

Above: Hood pins were a $16.55 option on the 1971 Charger.

Right: In 1971, Dodge adapted the Plymouth Air Grabber system for the new Charger. It was standard with the Hemi engine.

Below: Dodge designers incorporated a halo rear bumper into the design of the 1971 Charger.

Plymouth designers did an excellent job in the restyling of its 1971 B-body cars. The Belvedere series was replaced by the Satellite series, which included the GTX and Road Runner. This new rounded body theme became known as a "fuselage" design, because of its similarity to an aircraft fuselage. The new Road Runners and GTX models were only offered as two-door hardtops. The only convertible in Plymouth's catalog of cars in 1971 was the Barracuda.

1971 Road Runner Prices

Two-door hardtop: $3,120

Hemi engine: $883.55

Four-speed transmission: $206.40

TorqueFlite transmission: $ 237.50

Bucket seats: $105.95

The best way to identify a 1971 Hemi Road Runner was by the small HEMI decal on the front fender.

Plymouth offered optional front and rear bumpers painted body color.

In addition to the Hemi engine, the 1971 Road Runner's engine compartment included the lavender-colored beep-beep horn.

In 1971, when Dodge dropped the aging Coronet series, it smartly created the Super Bee out of the Charger. This provided Dodge with an entry-level intermediate that would compete with the Mercury Cyclone and Pontiac GTO. Dodge retained the Charger's body, but added doors without the Charger's two vertical imitation louvers. The body stripe patterns were the same for the Charger R/T and the Super Bee.

1971 Charger Super Bee Prices

Two-door hardtop: $3,271

Hemi engine: $883.55

Four-speed transmission: $206.40

Bucket seats: $105.95

Rallye wheels: $58.95

G60x15 raised white-letter tires: $63.10

Right: Front and rear spoilers were optional on both the 1971 Charger R/T and the Super Bee.

Left: All 1971 Charger Super Bees received this black hood decal.

Below: An extra heavy-duty suspension was included with the Hemi engine on the 1971 Charger Super Bee.

The Hemi engine option for the 1971 Dodge Charger R/T cost an extra $746.50. Dodge built a total of 2,659 Charger R/Ts in 1971 with 63 of those being Hemi powered (33 TorqueFlite and 30 four-speed). A four-speed manual transmission was included as standard equipment with the TorqueFlite as an option. The Hemi engine could not be ordered with air conditioning, speed control, or a three-speed manual transmission. Also standard with the Hemi engine was the extra heavy-duty suspension and dual exhaust. A Track Pak rear axle package was optional for the Hemi along with a Super Track Pak, both of which included the bulletproof Dana rear axle.

> *1971 Hemi Charger R/T Specs*
> **Weight with Hemi engine: 4,083 pounds**
> **0 to 60 acceleration: 5.7 seconds**
> **Quarter-mile elapsed time: 13.73 seconds**
> **Quarter-mile speed: 104 miles per hour**
> **Gas mileage: 11–12 miles per gallon**

All 1971 Hemi-powered Charger R/T and Super Bees used an oval shaped air cleaner that was painted orange with black HEMI lettering on top.

The Pistol Grip shifter was so named because it had the look and feel of custom-made grips for a handgun.

The bodyside stripes were standard for all 1971 Charger R/Ts. They were only available in black and could be deleted.

The 1971 Plymouth Road Runner and GTX shared the same basic body chassis and interior components. Plymouth positioned the GTX as an upscale muscle car, while the Road Runner filled the niche as its street fighter. This was similar to the market positioning of Dodge's Charger R/T and Super Bee. Plymouth's showroom competition for these two cars was Ford's Torino and Chevrolet's SS Chevelle. Of the two, the 1971 Torino had the freshest styling, but neither car could match the engine lineup offered by Plymouth, especially the Hemi.

Hemi Fact

In 1971, Plymouth sold 13,046 Road Runners. Most were equipped with the 300-horsepower 383. Also available was the 275-horsepower 340 and the Six Barrel 440 rated at 390 horsepower. But only 55 Hemi-powered Road Runners were sold in 1971.

Right: Vinyl bucket seats were a $105.95 option on the 1971 Road Runner. The console cost an extra $57.65.

Left: The engine code for a Hemi on a 1971 Road Runner's fender tag is "R."

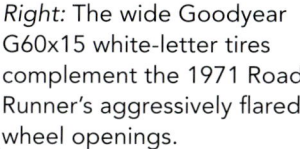

Right: The wide Goodyear G60x15 white-letter tires complement the 1971 Road Runner's aggressively flared wheel openings.

Dodge's best-selling 1971 Charger was its SE version. This model offered the best of Dodge's long list of luxury options and accessories. This car was not designed as a street racer, but as a comfortable boulevard cruiser. Dodge included a vinyl roof in black, white, green, or gold. A split-back bench seat was standard, but leather-covered bucket seats were optional. Hidden headlights were also a standard feature. The standard engine for the SE Charger was the 318-ci engine. But a 375-horsepower 440 Magnum V-8 could be ordered. The 1971 Charger SE was a glimpse into the future where style and comfort would outweigh horsepower.

Hemi Fact

On the NASCAR tracks in 1971, Bobby Isaac, driver of the K&K Insurance–sponsored 1971 Charger, was the most successful Dodge driver, but only won two races. He was the winner of the Firecracker 400 at Daytona Beach and the Old Dominion 500 at Martinsville, Virginia. Richard Petty was more successful in his Road Runner that won 21 races and his first Winston Cup Championship.

The Hemi engine in this low-mileage 1971 Charger R/T survivor has never been out of the car.

Dodge also offered its stylish Road Wheels as an option on the 1971 Charger R/T.

Hidden headlights were an available option on the 1971 Charger R/T.

Chapter 5

1970s E-Body Hemi Cars

By the time 1970 arrived, the muscle car party was in full swing. Plenty to drink and eat and the band had the amps cranked to full volume. Unfortunately, the cranky neighbors and insurance underwriters were about to close it down. The party only lasted for a few years, but they were the most memorable ones of the era. But Chrysler wasn't going to let the party end without introducing its fashionably late E-body Dodge Challengers and Plymouth Barracudas.

Prior to 1970, Plymouth's Barracuda and performance 'Cuda model could not compete with Chevrolet's Camaro or Ford's Mustang. Dodge didn't even have a pony car to sell. Chrysler's success with its 1968 and 1969 models gave it the cash to develop an all-new pony car for both Dodge and Plymouth. Chrysler's engineers were able to take the B-body's cowl and mate it to these highly styled pony cars. The B-body cowl gave the product planners carte blanche on their selection of engines. This meant that the powerful Hemi would be on the option list. Plymouth called its performance version of the Barracuda simply 'Cuda; and Dodge added its familiar R/T designation to its performance-based Challenger.

Hemi car collector Harold Sullivan is adding the final details to the Hemi engine that will be installed in the 1971 Hemi 'Cuda convertible in the background.

Hemi 'Cuda convertibles are the rarest of the breed. At the recent Barrett-Jackson auction, a 1970s model like this one fetched a staggering $2 million.

The new 1970 Challenger R/T and 'Cuda were pony car lover's dreams. They were beautifully styled and offered a long list of options that included leather interiors, heavy-duty suspension packages, and aggressive stripes. Each engine option included a host of complimentary heavy-duty components that ensured there were no weak links that could lead to failure. Included with the Hemi 'Cuda and optional on a Challenger R/T with a Hemi engine was the new Shaker hood scoop. It was Chrysler's equivalent of a bully poking the nose of every other muscle car on the street. To showcase its new E-body cars, Chrysler quickly got involved with the Sports Car Club of America's (SCCA) Trans-Am series and the National Hot Rod Association's (NHRA) new Pro Stock class.

Dodge and Plymouth designers gave the 1971 Challengers and Barracudas a light facelift. The most noticeable of changes was the front end of the 'Cuda with its new grille and front fender gills. Plymouth's design team also gave the 'Cuda the largest and boldest engine callout stripes ever seen with the billboard stripes that covered the entire quarter panel and half the door. The Challenger received a new grille and taillights. The R/T models were also given an aggressive set of body scoops that attached in front of the rear wheels.

But as 1971 dawned, the automotive insurance industry started to cast a larger and more ominous shadow. The cost of insuring a muscle car, especially one with a Hemi engine, became exceptionally high. In addition, new federal emissions laws were going to have a detrimental effect on the future of the muscle car phenomenon. Those considering buying a new Hemi 'Cuda had to figure in the high insurance payments as well as the cost of the expensive Hemi engine option. More often than not, the buyer would select a smaller engine. Muscle cars and street racing had lost their importance. As the muscle car era ended at the end of the 1971 model year, so too did the reign of the 426-ci street Hemi.

Plymouth designers discretely added a small "hemicuda" emblem to the Shaker hood scoop of each 1970 and 1971 Hemi 'Cuda

Plymouth introduced its all-new Barracuda in 1970. To save money, Chrysler's product planners dictated the use of the B-body cowl and K-member. This resulted in a performance benefit because it allowed for the installation of Chrysler's complete suite of engines including the Hemi. The wide engine compartment also added to the width of the car, giving it a more aggressive look. Performance-based Barracudas were called "'Cudas," a street slang derived from Barracuda. The Hemi engine could only be ordered in 'Cuda trim.

Hemi Fact

If asked, the average automotive enthusiast would say that all 'Cudas came with bucket seats. While bucket seats were popular, Plymouth also offered a split-bench seat with a fold-down center armrest for the 'Cuda. The only restriction with this option was the requirement of an automatic transmission.

Above: Plymouth's product planners offered a multitude of options for the 1970 'Cuda including a bench seat and column-shifted TorqueFlite automatic transmission.

Left: All 1970 Hemi 'Cudas were fitted with the Shaker hood scoop. In addition to black, it was also available in argent, and a few selected body colors.

Below: The standard wheels for any 1970 'Cuda were body-color steel wheels with small "dog dish" hubcaps.

In 1970, Dodge Division released its first pony car–the Challenger. Like the Barracuda, it was offered in several levels of trim with the R/T as the performance version and the SE as the luxury version. These two options could be combined as seen on this R/T SE Challenger. Dodge product planners also added a wide range of economy and performance engines to the new 1970 Challenger. Complementing each engine package were a wide range of heavy-duty chassis standard features.

1970 Challenger Dimensions
Wheelbase: 110 inches
Overall length: 191.3 inches
Width: 76.1 inches
Front track: 59.7 inches
Rear track: 60.7 inches

A standard feature on each Hemi-equipped 1970 Challenger R/T was a set of Goodyear G70-14 Polyglas white-letter tires.

Dodge Challengers with the Hemi engine were not fitted with the Shaker hood scoop—it was optional.

The 1970 Challengers with the SE option featured a special vinyl top that included a smaller rear window. Also included with the SE option is the small SE emblem at the lower corner of the C-pillar.

1970 'Cuda Dimensions
Wheelbase: 108 inches
Overall length: 186.6 inches
Width: 74.9 inches
Front track: 59.7 inches
Rear track: 60.7 inches

Above: The small black rear-deck spoiler was part of the 1970 All American Racers (AAR) 'Cuda option. The owner of this Hemi 'Cuda added it along with a 426 Hemi emblem.

Left: Plymouth engineers fitted the 1970 Hemi 'Cuda's Shaker hood scoop with a rubber gasket to seal it against the bottom of the hood. Because of its size, the Shaker scoop could not be added to any car with air conditioning.

Below: An available option for the 1970 Hemi 'Cuda was leather-covered bucket seats.

Opposite: Plymouth's 1970 Barracuda and performance-based 'Cudas included the latest in automotive design trends, including hidden windshield wipers. Plymouth designers accomplished hiding these necessary components by slightly lowering the cowl and raising the rear of the hood. The slots in the rear of the hood allow airflow to the passenger compartment. Like all 1970 Hemi 'Cudas, this one's equipped with the Shaker hood scoop.

Dodge designers were not required to use any of the Barracuda's body components when they designed the 1970 Challenger. This gave them an exceptional amount of control to design a car that had a family resemblance to the Barracuda without restrictions. Dodge also stretched the wheelbase by 2 inches over the Barracuda which gave their Challenger slightly different proportions.

1970 Challenger R/T Prices
Challenger R/T hardtop: $3,266
Challenger R/T convertible: $3,535
Challenger R/T SE hardtop: $3,498
Hemi engine: $778.75
Shaker hood scoop: $97.30

Left: The Shaker hood scoop was an option on all 1970 Hemi-powered Challengers. This Shaker was also specified in the body color of Plum Crazy.

Below: All 1970 Challenger R/T models were fitted with these special exhaust tips that extended through the bottom of the rear valence panel.

The styling of the 1970 Plymouth Barracuda was exceptionally clean and free of excessive frills. The sides were slightly bulged with an aggressive rise in the quarter panels over the rear wheels. Plymouth designers also bucked the trend of quad headlights and installed large single headlights at each end of the grille opening. Flush door handles were another feature of the Barracuda design. 'Cuda models were fitted with standard hood pins and driving lights.

Hemi Fact

The Hemi 'Cuda's Shaker hood scoop featured internal baffles that closed off the opening to prevent rain or snow from entering. These baffles could be opened by the pull of a lever that was mounted on the lower edge of the instrument panel.

Above: Hockey Stick stripes were optional for the 1970 'Cuda with an engine callout added to the end. These stripes were only available in black.

Above: While the Shaker hood scoop looked impressive while driving down the street, it covered much of the engine when the hood was open.

Right: Plymouth painted the taillight panel on all 1970 'Cudas a low-gloss black. This same panel on a Barracuda was painted body color.

Dodge designers created a large grille opening for the 1970 Dodge Challenger. The deep-set grille features a Challenger emblem and an R/T emblem (on R/T models). All R/T models featured hood pins. Dodge designers initially wanted to do a complete halo bumper on the Challenger, but cost restraints only allowed a thin chrome molding across the tops of the fenders and the leading edge of the hood. The Challenger's hunched quarter panels are accentuated by the body's character line that rises over the rear wheel opening.

Hemi Fact

When Chrysler designed the new 1970 Dodge Challenger (and Barracuda) body they built it with unibody construction. Chrysler was one of the pioneers of this type of construction where the entire body structure is welded into a single rigid unit. This creates an exceptionally solid body that offers better handling and ride qualities.

The ad copy in image:

Dodge

This Pony has Horses...
1970 Dodge Challenger R/T

1970's all-new high-performance pony car. It borrowed from no one. Completely new from the wide stance up. And the scoop drops the hint. The pony has a mean streak. Like a 383 Magnum V8. Light it up, and you'll get a quaking trace of four-barrel thunder. Or things get a mite stormier with the optional 440 Magnum V8 . . . or the all-out "haulin' Hemi." Challenger R/T has all the other going goodies, too: 3-on-the-floor full-synchro manual transmission • HD drum-type brakes • Wide-tread tires • Rallye Suspension with sway bar • Rallye Instrument Cluster • Bright dual exhaust tips • 3.23 axle ratio • New longitudinal stripe or traditional bumblebee stripe (your choice) • Brand-new optional 440 SixPack— three Holley two-barrels on a new high-rise manifold, vibrating under the new shaker hood (an option soon to be available). 1970 Dodge Challenger R/T. Kind of "cute" . . . 'til you let out the horses.

Dodge Scat Pack . . . the cars with the Bumblebee stripes

Right: In 1970, Dodge wasn't hesitant to advertise the performance capability of its new Hemi Challenger R/T.

Left: Dodge fitted all of its 1970 Hemi Challenger R/T models with Rallye wheels and white-letter Goodyear tires.

Right: The 1970 Challenger R/T customer had the option of adding this side stripe or deleting it in favor of emblems. The racing-style gas cap was a standard Challenger R/T item.

Plymouth designers made very few changes to the exterior sheet metal of the 1971 Barracuda. The most dramatic change they made was to the grille. They added quad headlights and added six apertures to create what is affectionately called the "cheese grater." This new grille could also be painted body color. There was also a small change to the taillights. The other distinctive feature the designers added to the 1971 'Cuda models are the front fender gills.

Hemi Fact

In 1971, Plymouth only offered two transmissions with its Hemi engine: a four-speed manual with a Hurst Pistol Grip shifter, or a TorqueFlite automatic. With the Hemi, the TorqueFlite cost an additional $229.35.

Above: Plymouth only added the gills to the 'Cuda in 1971. There were four on each side and they were nonfunctional.

Left: The engine callout for the 1971 'Cudas, Billboard stripes were placed on the doors.

Below: In 1971, Plymouth added Billboard stripes–the largest stripes to ever be added to the side of a muscle car. They were available in either white or black.

One nice addition to the 1971 'Cuda model was the expansion of the elastomeric bumper option. These bumpers were available in limited colors on 1970 'Cudas, but not available on 1970 Challengers or Challenger R/Ts. But in 1971, a wider selection of body-colored elastomeric front and rear bumpers were available. While this 1971 'Cuda has the body-colored elastomeric front bumper, its grille is the standard argent color. This mixing and matching of components and long list of options gave the customer the ability to create a highly personalized car.

> **Hemi Fact**
>
> Dodge division also built Hemi-powered Challenger R/Ts in 1971, but in much smaller numbers than the 'Cudas. Only 71 Hemi-powered Challenger R/Ts were built and these were all hardtops. Dodge did not offer the R/T option on the convertible.

Right: The Shaker hood scoop was a standard item on the 1971 Hemi 'Cuda.

Left: Plymouth offered attractive leather coverings for the 1971 'Cuda's high-back bucket seats.

Below: This 1971 Hemi 'Cuda is fitted with the optional luggage rack.

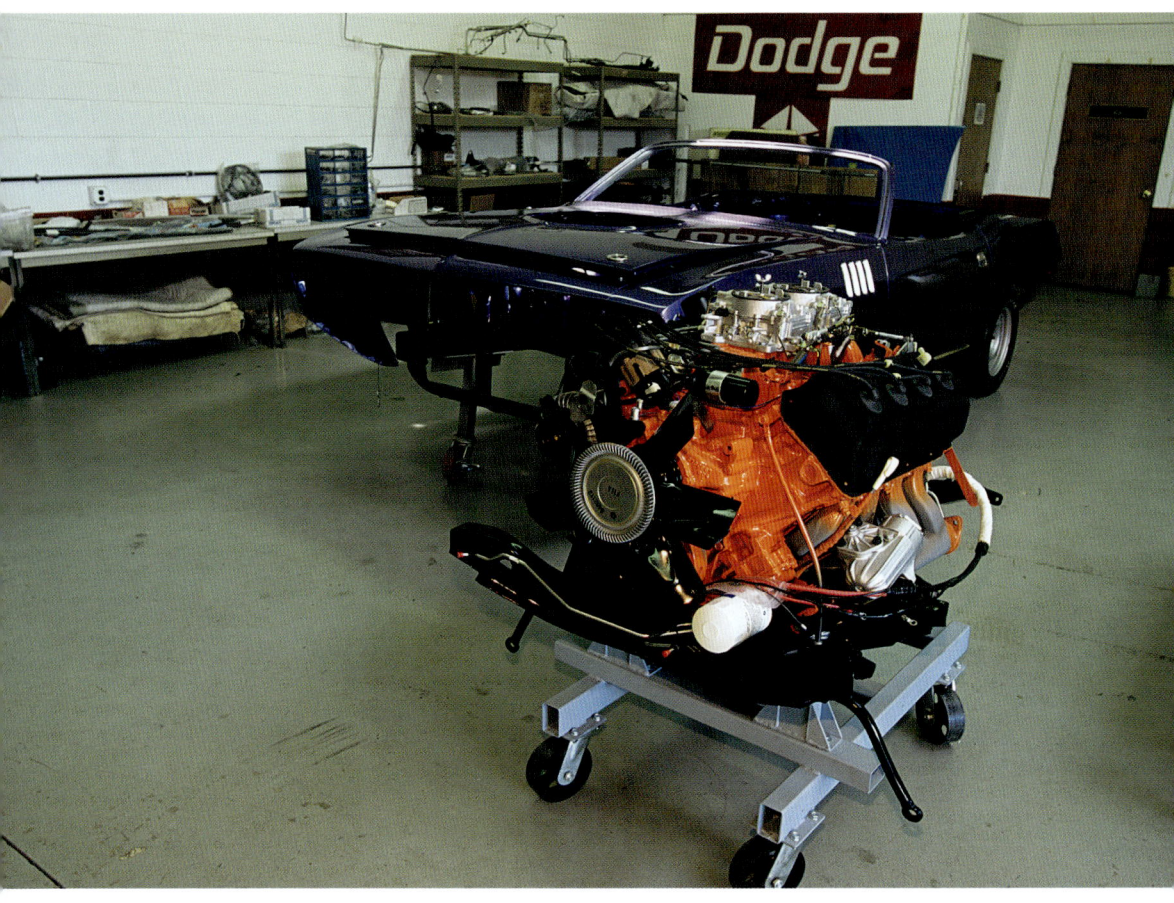

The 426 street Hemi engine Chrysler installed in its 1971 models was basically the same engine it first installed in 1966. The biggest change was the addition of hydraulic lifters in 1970. All street Hemi engines were painted Hemi Orange with the massive valve covers painted Crinkle Black. This engine has been completely rebuilt, was highly detailed, and is destined for the 1971 'Cuda convertible body in the background. On the assembly line, Chrysler first mounted its engines on the K-member and decked (installed) them from below. Because of its width, the Hemi was the most difficult engine to install.

Hemi Engine Specs
Bore: 4.25 inches
Stroke: 3.75 inches
Displacement: 426 cubic inches
Compression ratio: 10.25:1
Horsepower: 425 @ 5000
Torque: 490 ft-lbs @ 4000

Above: Chrysler mounted the Hemi's mechanical fuel pump on the right-hand side of the engine along with the alternator. All Chrysler street Hemi engines were equipped with a thermostatic fan.

Right: All street Hemi engines were equipped with a pair of Carter AFB four-barrel carburetors.

Below: The street Hemi's right-hand exhaust manifold gracefully swept rearward.

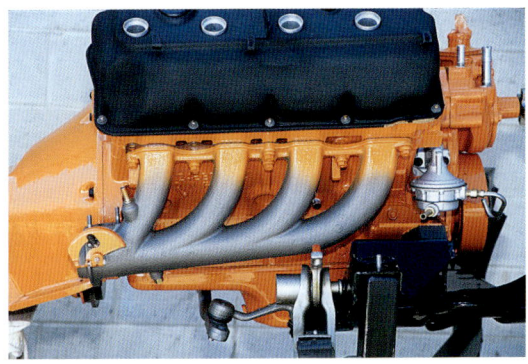

In 1971, the muscle/pony car market was in a steep downward spiral. Chrysler had invested a lot of money to bring out its new E-body Barracuda and Challenger models and was now being challenged by Chevrolet and Ford. When first introduced in 1970, they were the hottest cars on the street. But Chevrolet, albeit late, introduced its restyled 1970 Camaro, and in 1971 Ford released its completely restyled Mustang. In addition, the auto insurance companies were exerting their own form of muscle with surcharges for those who decided that a big block was a necessary option. In addition, new federal emissions regulations were on the horizon that would drive a wooden stake through the heart of the muscle car movement. In addition to being the last year for the Hemi, 1971 was also the last year for the Barracuda convertible.

> *1971 'Cuda Prices*
> Base 'Cuda coupe: $3,134
> Base 'Cuda convertible: $3,391
> Hemi engine: $883.90
> Leather bucket seats: $62.55
> AM/FM stereo radio: $196.60

Above: Keeping a Hemi engine running in top form took a moderate amount of mechanical knowledge and a good deal of time.

Right: In addition to the Billboard stripes, this highly optioned 1971 Hemi 'Cuda also has the rear window louvers, black vinyl top (required with the louvers), and Go Wing.

Plymouth's product planners marketed the 1971 Barracuda in the same way Ford did with the Mustang. Plymouth offered two body styles, a coupe and a convertible, that could be purchased with many different options allowing the buyer to create a car that would be totally unique. Plymouth's long list of options for the Barracuda gave the customer the ability to purchase a fully loaded Barracuda with a small engine, or a stripped-down 'Cuda with a Hemi. This Hemi 'Cuda is one of those stripped-down models. That's confirmed by only one exterior rearview mirror.

1971 'Cuda Production Numbers
'Cuda hardtops: 5,314
'Cuda convertibles: 293
Hemi 'Cuda hardtops: 108
Hemi 'Cuda convertibles: 17
Total Barracuda and 'Cuda production: 16,159

Above: The painted wheels and dog dish hubcaps may have fooled a few would-be racers on the street into believing this 'Cuda was powered by something other than a Hemi.

Left: All 1971 Hemi 'Cudas were equipped with the Shaker hood scoop. Plymouth offered it as an option with other engines.

Below: Vinyl tops were very popular in 1971 and only added an additional $82.40 to the sticker price of this 1971 Hemi 'Cuda.

Chapter 6

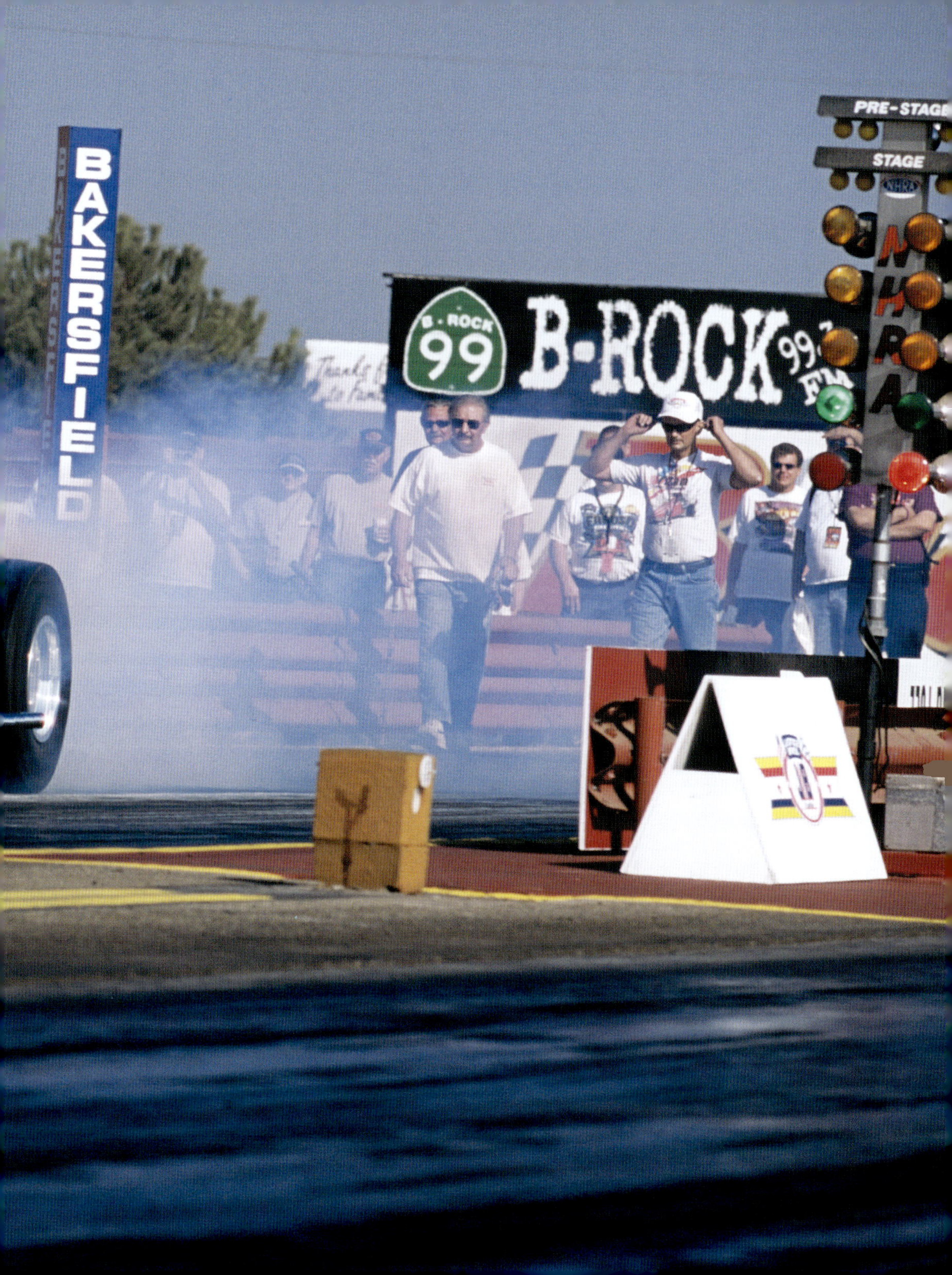

BAKERSFIELD
B-ROCK
99
B-ROCK
PRE-STAGE
STAGE
NHRA

Hemi Hot Rods & Drag Racers

Chrysler's Hemi engine has provided the power for hot rods, drag racers, and circle track racers for decades. Its efficient combustion chambers and excellent breathing capability were among the reasons hot rodders and racers of all kinds loved it so passionately. Its ability to create high levels of horsepower is the single reason why NASCAR ultimately legislated it out of competition. Early drag racers loved the first-generation Hemi and quickly found ways to increase its horsepower. It was the engine of choice for all the Top Fuel dragsters in the 1950s and 1960s. The second-generation 426 Hemi found a home in Super Stock race cars, which quickly morphed into Funny Cars. Today, every Top Fuel dragster and Funny Car runs a Hemi engine.

Hot rodders who first ran the flathead V-8 were the early implementers of the new overhead-valve V-8 engines. They would scour junkyards looking for a late-model Cadillac or Oldsmobile wreck and extract the new V-8 engine for their jalopies. Hot rodders tried every new V-8 as it became available. By 1955, with the release of the Chrysler C-300 with its 300-horsepower engine, they figured out which new V-8 engine was going to give them the most horsepower.

In 1965, Dodge upped the ante for drag racers by producing a limited number of altered-wheelbase cars that soon became known as Funny Cars.

In the mid-1960s, the Chrysler Hemi was the preferred powerplant for Top Fuel dragsters. The headers on this dragster are called "weed burners" for obvious reasons.

In the mid-1950s, drag racers were experimenting with a new style of car—the slingshot dragster. These cars were stripped down with the driver, and his additional weight load, riding over the rear axle for added traction. Oklahoman Melvin Heath built his own dragster, and added a Chrysler Hemi engine. He proceeded to win the Top Eliminator title at the 1956 NHRA National Championship Drag Races with an elapsed time of 10.49 seconds and a speed of 141.50 miles per hour. Don Garlits, the most famous drag racer of all time, started out with a flathead-powered dragster that he towed to the track behind a Chrysler 1940 Ford coupe powered by a Hemi. As soon as he realized that his tow car was quicker than his dragster, he swapped engines. In 1956, he built the first of his many *Swamp Rat* dragsters; with only one exception, each dragster was powered by a Chrysler Hemi. By the mid-1960s, Top Fuel

dragsters were the best show in drag racing. This period has often been called the "Golden Era of Drag Racing" because of the number of Top Fuel dragsters competing. Chrysler's Hemi was the most popular engine in these dragsters then, as it is today.

Chrysler's return to NASCAR in 1964 with a new 426 Hemi engine also meant that drag racers would have the latest in Hemi technology. Hemi-powered Super Stock racers dominated the class. The popularity of match racing led to a "run what you brung" tradition, where competitors altered the car's wheelbase and added fuel injection and blowers. These modified cars were called "funny cars" because of their odd proportions and were the precursor of today's 330-mile-per-hour Funny Cars.

The Chrysler Hemi engine has been a mainstay in racing since its creation. It provided dominating power first on the NASCAR tracks in the mid-1950s and then again in the mid-1960s. Because of its ability to make almost unlimited horsepower, it is the only engine used for all of today's Top Fuel and Funny Car racers.

Mr. Norm was the Chicago area's premier high-performance Dodge dealer. This full-page ad is for the 1965 A-990 Hemi race cars Dodge built.

Hot rodding was born on the dry lakebeds of Southern California. It was there that young men would take their roadsters to be timed for speed. The fenders would be stripped off and the cars would run the dusty track at full throttle. Initially, the favorite engine of the racers was the V-8 Ford flathead. It was plentiful, inexpensive, and aftermarket manufacturers offered a large supply of speed equipment. Hot rodders sat up and took notice when the major auto manufacturers started to build overhead V-8s in the 1950s. The early Hemi's ability to make lots of horsepower made it a favorite of hot rodders.

> *Hot Rod Fact*
>
> The 1932 Ford Roadster has become the iconic American hot rod. In 1932, Henry Ford was the first to build a low-cost V-8. The cars he built that year were not made-over Model As, but completely brand-new vehicles. Most of the Ford body styles were made completely of steel while all of Ford's competitors were still using wood to support the exterior steel panels.

Left: This Dodge Red Ram Hemi engine fits nicely in the 1932 Ford's engine compartment.

Below: The 1932 Ford Roadster is the favorite of hot rodders because of its classic style and excellent proportions.

Hot rodders have always liked Ford products. They were durable and plentiful, which meant they were also inexpensive. Between 1928 and 1931, Ford built millions of Model As such as this 1931 coupe. One modification that hot rodders applied to their cars for both appearance and a slight performance gain, was to chop the top. This "lowering of the lid" balanced the proportions of the body and slightly reduced aerodynamic drag. Hot rodders also mixed and matched parts in creating their cars. In addition to the vintage Hemi engine, this Model A body is riding on a 1932 Ford frame and also has a 1932 Ford grille shell. The only rule in hot rodding is that there are no rules.

Hemi Hot Rod Components

In the 1950s, as hot rodders became interested in V-8 engines other than the Ford flathead, the aftermarket component manufacturers sat up and took notice. These companies had cut their technological teeth on flathead speed equipment and now they would take that catalog of knowledge and apply it to the new Hemi V-8s. Soon there were aluminum multi-carburetor intake manifolds to improve performance and finned aluminum valve covers for appearance.

Right: This Hemi is decked out with several polished aluminum aftermarket components.

Left: A chopped top leaves little room inside this Model A hot rod.

Right: A louvered deck lid and 1939 Ford taillights are traditional hot rod features.

Heath's 1956 NHRA Championship–winning dragster was built over a period of three months in the implement shed on his farm. It, like many of the mid-1950s dragsters, had the look of a modified sprint car, with the driver sitting back over the rear axle. Heath constructed the frame out of chrome-moly tubing and used a 1937 Ford front axle. Gear ratios in the 1940 Ford rear axle were either 4.11 or 3.78. Recap slicks were fitted to the rear. The Heath-built sheetmetal body was crudely constructed without the aid of templates. The Chrysler Hemi engine Heath installed featured JE pistons, a Chet Herbert cam, and oversize valves. The Crower U-FAB log intake manifold mounts six Stromberg 97 carburetors. The power from the nitro-burning Hemi was transmitted through a 1939 Ford transmission. While winning the 1956 NHRA Top Eliminator title, Heath ran an elapsed time of 10.49 seconds at a speed of 141.50 miles per hour. The entire cost of Heath's championship dragster was $1,000—half the cost of a new Chevy Bel Air in 1956.

Drag Racing Fact

In 1956, organized drag racing was in its infancy. The NHRA had just been established to provide racers a safe venue in which to race. At that time there were no purpose-built drag strips, only converted World War II military airstrips. The distance of a quarter-mile was established as the length of a drag race because of the length of the airstrips that would allow plenty of space to slow down after the finish line.

Right: Stromberg 97 carburetors were the racer's choice in 1956.

Left: The small silver-colored cylinder on the side of the cowl is a pump that pressurizes the fuel tank to ensure fuel flow to the carburetors.

Right: The only drag slicks available in 1956 were recapped street tires.

When Don Garlits first built his *Swamp Rat I*, drag chutes had not been used to slow dragsters from the high speeds they attained.

Garlits' big nitro-burning Hemi ran with eight Stromberg 97 carburetors.

The *Swamp Rat I* was the first of a long string of Garlits' *Swamp Rat* dragsters. Most all were black and most were exceptionally fast.

Opposite: Don Garlits' *Swamp Rat I* dragster put him on drag racing's map as a star attraction. The foundation for this car was a pair of 1930 Chevrolet frame rails that he found in a junkyard. Powering Garlits' dragster would be a Chrysler Hemi engine. Internally, it was balanced, ported, and polished, and ran an Isky cam. On top were eight Stromberg 97 carburetors on a Weiand Drag Star aluminum manifold. Garlits painted his dragster a sinister shade of black with red and white pin striping. In building the *Swamp Rat I*, Garlits realized that a dragster should be built from the ground up, not from a converted hot rod. He also knew a successful dragster needed a low center of gravity, a streamlined shape, and maximum weight over the rear wheels for optimum traction.

Don Garlits Fact

Don Garlits is a living legend with an enormous amount of drive that keeps him young. Garlits has no concept of retiring, with his feet up watching television. In 2001, the NHRA named him as the top drag racer of all time. He added an exclamation point to that honor by qualifying for the 2001 U.S. Nationals, in a borrowed car, with a personal best of 303.37 miles per hour in 4.720 seconds.

In the late 1950s and early 1960s, one of the hottest A/Altered coupes was *Walt's Puffer II*. It was a blown Hemi Chrysler-powered 1939 Fiat, built in 1959 by Walt Knoch and Tom Redmond. Knoch owned Walt's Auto Parts in Inkster, Michigan, and the car's home track was the nearby Detroit Dragway. On its very first run at the 1959 U.S. Nationals, *Walt's Puffer* broke the class record for speed with a run of 138.67 miles per hour. By 1960, *Walt's Puffer* was running speeds of 150 miles per hour, with elapsed times in the 10-second range. In 1962, *Walt's Puffer II* won the A/Altered class and Knoch's roadster *Walt's Puffer Too* won the A/Roadster class. The two cars were to be in the final for the Junior Eliminator title, but a rainstorm moved in. With only the two *Walt's Puffer* cars to run against each other, it was assured that one of Knoch's cars would win. The trophy was awarded to Knoch and the books record *Walt's Puffers* as the winners—first and second.

Drag Racing Fact

The nose-high attitude of the *Walt's Puffer* Fiat is attributable to a 1960s theory for increased traction. This theory dictated that since the front end of a car rises upon acceleration transferring weight to the rear wheels, why not save the horsepower it takes to raise it by building it with the front end raised. There may have been a slight increase in traction, but the raised nose certainly hurt top speed.

Right: A gentleman who did sheetmetal heater ducting for a living made the injector scoop on *Walt's Puffer.*

Below: The Hemi engine in the *Walt's Puffer* Fiat ran on pump gas, as required by NHRA rules.

Lower right: The steering wheel on *Walt's Puffer* is from a Corvette. The only gauge is for oil pressure.

Races between nitro-burning altered coupes and roadsters were spectacles that took place in the late 1950s and early 1960s, primarily in Southern California. Gene Mooneyham had been a regular, running his coupe as fast as 120 miles per hour until an accident at San Diego's Paradise Mesa drag strip convinced Mooneyham that he should retire from driving. When he rebuilt his coupe he chopped the top, added a supercharger to the Chrysler Hemi engine, and asked Larry Faust to drive. Lettered on the side of the blue coupe were the numbers 554—numbers that would soon be famous. The *Mooneyham 554* coupe consistently ranked first on the *Drag News* Jr. Eliminator list. It was constantly booked for match races and challenges for the number one spot on that list. The fans loved Mooneyham's coupe and would turn out to see the tire-smoking duels between it and its challenger. Eventually, it was sold and Mooneyham moved on to fuel dragsters.

Fuel Coupe Fact

The *Mooneyham 554* coupe was in a distinct class of cars that ran primarily on the West Coast. The NHRA did not recognize these fuel coupes, because they ran nitromethane instead of gasoline. These cars were exceptionally loud and ran the length of the quarter-mile on the edge of control while smoking the tires. The fans loved the match races the promoters booked because the races were so exciting.

The big nitro-burning Chrysler Hemi in *Mooneyham's 554* coupe was the same engine used in Top Fuel dragsters.

While the outside of Mooneyham's coupe looked like a hot rod, the interior was pure race car.

The *Mooneyham 554* 1934 Ford coupe had a traditional hot rod stance that Southern California drag racing fans loved.

David Newhard

In addition to releasing the Hemi engine for NASCAR racing in 1964, Chrysler also released a special version for drag racing. The cars Chrysler used were the lightest two-door sedans Plymouth and Dodge produced. In addition, they took additional weight out of the cars by the use of lightweight materials and by simply reducing the amount of parts in the car. Unnecessary items like the rear seat, sun visors, and armrests were deleted. Most cars were built with the TorqueFlite automatic, but a few were equipped with a four-speed.

Hemi Fact

In 1964, drag racing's sanctioning bodies did not restrict the amount of carburetors a manufacturer could place on an engine. For the Hemi drag race cars, Chrysler used the short cross-ram intake that was similar to the one used on its Max Wedge engines. It mounted a pair of Holley four-barrel carburetors.

The race Hemi engine Chrysler installed into its 1964 drag race sedans was only rated at 425 horsepower. *David Newhardt*

Right: The bare-bones interior on Chrysler's 1964 drag race cars consisted of two lightweight bucket seats. *David Newhardt*

On January 21, 1963, four Southern California kids joined up and created an unforgettable drag racing team. Ron Rivero, Norm Weekly, Jim Fox, and Dennis Holding decided to campaign a dragster. They soon became known as the "Frantic Four"— a name derived from the incredible performance they got out of their 354-ci Chrysler engine (most competitors were running the 392-ci Hemi) and the attitude all four of them had toward racing. In 1963, they established several track records on the West Coast and the reputation of the Frantic Four soon spread across the nation. The team's accomplishments included a 202.24-mile-per-hour top speed of the meet at the 1964 U.S. Nationals. They also held the *Drag News* #1 Fuel Spot with victories over drag racing legends Don Garlits, Don Prudhomme, and Chris Karamesines.

Frantic Four Fact

The original Frantic Four dragster has long since disappeared. The one in these photographs is a re-creation of the original that was built in 2001 by Rob Peppmuller, who also built this one. Today, the same group of four friends that campaigned the original car take this beautiful re-creation to car shows where it's regularly fired off.

Above: The only way to start a dragster is by pushing it with another vehicle because dragsters do not have onboard starters.

Left: While most other dragsters ran the larger 392-ci Hemi engine, the Frantic Four used the smaller 354-ci Hemi engine in their dragster.

Below: "Stormin'" Norman Weekly, the Frantic Four's driver, lights up the slicks.

For 1965, the specially built Dodges and Plymouths for the Chrysler drag racing program became known by their engineering code—A-990. For 1965, the NHRA dictated that cars designed for Super Stock competition could no longer substitute standard body panels for those of fiberglass or aluminum. Chrysler's engineers came up with a plan to comply with the rules, but still lighten the car as much as possible. They chose to remove everything from the car that was not required by federal or state law and to make the exterior sheet metal as thin as possible. The windshield was the only piece of real glass. All other windows were acrylic and the door hinges were made of aluminum. All A-990 cars were fitted with a tan vinyl interior—there were no other choices. These A-990 Dodges and Plymouths were exceptionally fast and dominated the Super Stock class in 1965.

Hemi Engine Fact

The engine powering the A-990 cars was Chrysler's race Hemi that had proven itself so well in 1964. Chrysler fitted the 1965 engine with aluminum heads while maintaining the 12.5:1 compression ratio. The only change Chrysler made to the cross-ram dual four-barrel intake manifold for 1965 was its material. The manifold was now cast from magnesium instead of aluminum.

Left: This 1965 print ad touts Dodge's supremacy of the Super Stock class with the race Hemi.

Lower Left: Chrysler's race Hemi engines were the only Hemis to come from the factory with chrome valve covers.

Below: The interior of all A-990 cars was trimmed in tan vinyl. This was the first year Chrysler did away with its fabled push-button drive.

Above: The upswept exhaust headers are called "zoomies." These were exceptionally popular on mid-1960s dragsters.

Upper Left: In the 1960s, dragster bodies were hand-formed out of aluminum.

Lower Left: The *Magicar's* body sweeps up in the rear, covering the roll bar and wrapping around the drag chute.

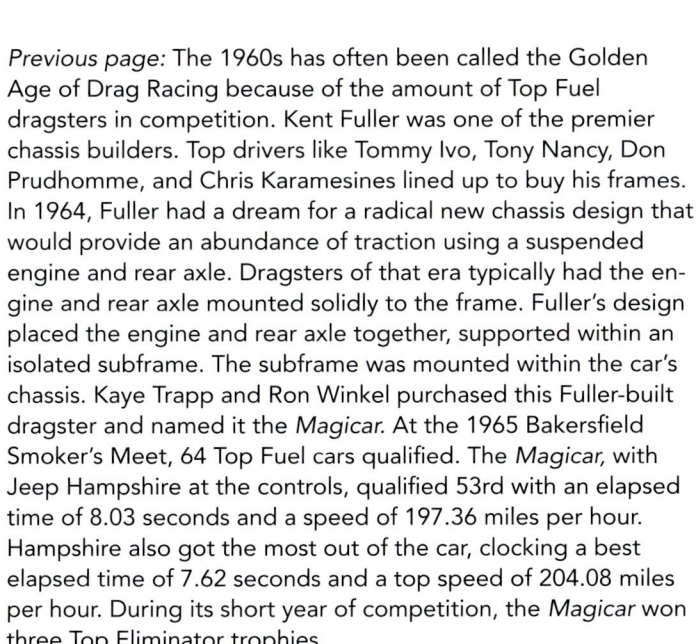

Previous page: The 1960s has often been called the Golden Age of Drag Racing because of the amount of Top Fuel dragsters in competition. Kent Fuller was one of the premier chassis builders. Top drivers like Tommy Ivo, Tony Nancy, Don Prudhomme, and Chris Karamesines lined up to buy his frames. In 1964, Fuller had a dream for a radical new chassis design that would provide an abundance of traction using a suspended engine and rear axle. Dragsters of that era typically had the engine and rear axle mounted solidly to the frame. Fuller's design placed the engine and rear axle together, supported within an isolated subframe. The subframe was mounted within the car's chassis. Kaye Trapp and Ron Winkel purchased this Fuller-built dragster and named it the *Magicar*. At the 1965 Bakersfield Smoker's Meet, 64 Top Fuel cars qualified. The *Magicar*, with Jeep Hampshire at the controls, qualified 53rd with an elapsed time of 8.03 seconds and a speed of 197.36 miles per hour. Hampshire also got the most out of the car, clocking a best elapsed time of 7.62 seconds and a top speed of 204.08 miles per hour. During its short year of competition, the *Magicar* won three Top Eliminator trophies.

> **Dragster Fact**
>
> In the mid-1960s, the Hemi engines used in dragsters developed approximately 1,000 horsepower. This type of horsepower was attained with a supercharger and by the use of nitromethane fuel. Because this fuel carries its own oxygen, it can be run in exceptionally rich mixtures.

In 1967, Chrysler once again built a series of cars specifically for the NHRA's Super Stock B class. To be legal for this class, Chrysler needed to build at least 50 production line vehicles. To fulfill the requirements, 55 Dodge Coronet 440 hardtops and 55 Plymouth Belvedere II hardtops were built. The Dodges were coded WO23 and the Plymouths, RO23. This special option included a standard-production 425-horsepower street Hemi engine and either a column-shifted TorqueFlite transmission with a special high-stall speed torque converter or a Hurst-shifted four-speed with an NHRA-approved explosion-proof bell housing. The automatic cars were equipped with a 4.86 Sure-Grip 8 3/4 rear end, and the four-speed cars were equipped with the Dana 4.88 Sure-Grip. These special Dodges and Plymouths were painted white with black bench seat interiors. These special Hemi cars were capable of running the quarter-mile in 11 seconds flat at a speed of 125 miles per hour and ended up owning NHRA's SS/B class.

Drag Racing Fact

As drag racing progressed through the early 1960s, the cars morphed from vehicles with high-performance engines that anyone could purchase, to altered-wheel-base Funny Cars run by professional racers. These cars no longer looked like anything in the showrooms. Chrysler's decision to build the WO23- and RO23-op-tioned cars, reflected what was available in the show-rooms. And the business of the automakers has always been to sell cars.

Above: For improved weight balance, Chrysler relocated the battery on all of the WO23- and RO23-optioned cars to the trunk.

Left: While the WO23 and RO23 bodies were stripped of any extra weight, the engines in these cars were standard-production street Hemi engines.

All WO23 and RO23 cars were fitted with the large hood scoop first seen on the 1964 Hemi Super Stock cars.

The 1968 Hemi Dodge Dart (and Plymouth Hemi Barracuda) was the brainchild of Chrysler's Dick Maxwell. Maxwell was a Chrysler engineer and Ramcharger club member. He felt the powerful race Hemi engine in the smaller A-body Dart would make an unbeatable drag car. Chrysler engineer Bob Tarrozi developed the specifications and built the prototype Barracuda. Both the Barracuda and Dart were built on the same platform, therefore the modifications made to shoehorn the big Hemi engine into the prototype Barracuda would be identical for the Dart. The most serious of these modifications was the reworking of the front spring towers and the special brake master cylinder. The rest of the modifications were designed to reduce the car's weight. The front fenders and hood, with its oversize scoop, were made of fiberglass. The body panels and bumpers were acid dipped to reduce the thickness of the metal. Deleted from the interior were the heater, radio, rear seat, all body insulation, and sound deadening material. The two small bucket seats were added from a Dodge van. All of the windows were made from a lightweight polymer.

> **Hemi Dart Fact**
>
> Chrysler contracted with the Hurst Corporation to build 50 Dodge Darts and 50 Plymouth Barracudas in the initial production run. Hurst opened a special facility in Hazel Park, Michigan, to build these cars. Later, an additional 25 of each car were produced, bringing total production for each car to 75 each. Many of these cars have survived and are currently racing.

Left: All of the Hemi Darts were shipped to the dealers with primer covering the metal body panels and the fiberglass front clip components in unpainted gel coat.

Right: Powering the 1968 Hemi Dart is Chrysler's famous race Hemi engine which featured 12.5:1 pistons, dual Holley carburetors on a magnesium cross ram intake manifold, an aluminum water pump, and Hooker exhaust headers.

Left: Dodge enlarged the rear wheel openings on the 1968 Hemi Darts to be able to accept large slicks.

In the early 1970s, Don Garlits built a series of rear-engine dragsters, some more successful than others. One of the most famous of Garlits' rear engine cars is *Swamp Rat 22*. It was the first dragster to go 250 miles per hour in a quarter-mile, an accomplishment other dragsters were unable to accomplish for seven years. In addition to the speed record, Garlits won both the International Hot Rod Association (IHRA) world title and the NHRA's World Championship in 1975 while driving the *Swamp Rat 22*.

Don Garlits Fact

In 1971, Don Garlits revolutionized drag racing when he introduced his *Swamp Rat 14*, drag racing's first successful rear-engine dragster. After an accident a year earlier where he lost part of his right foot, Garlits determined that sitting behind the engine was not the right place to be. Today, all Top Fuel dragsters are rear-engine design.

Above: Don Garlits' nickname, "Big Daddy," is painted on the front wing of his *Swamp Rat 22* dragster.

Left: Powering Garlits' *Swamp Rat 22* was a 480-ci Hemi engine with an estimated 2,500 horsepower.

Garlits' *Swamp Rat 22* debuted in the middle of the 1975 race season, replacing *Swamp Rat 21*. This new dragster had a 250-inch wheelbase and was 80 pounds lighter than its predecessor.

Don Prudhomme became a legendary dragster driver in the 1960s. As Funny Cars became more popular in the 1970s, he made the switch to this 'Cuda Funny Car. While not quite as fast as Top Fuel dragsters, the Funny Cars put on a spectacular show for the fans. The Funny Cars ran nitro, so they had the sound and fire of the Top Fuel dragsters. Showmanship was also part of the Funny Car extravaganza, including long smoky burnouts. Once the tire smoke cleared, they would rump-rump-rump back to the starting line, often with the aid of a scantily clad female. It was pure vaudeville with a large dose of good old American speed. Prudhomme raced this car at the 1973 U.S. Nationals and set a qualifying record with a time of 6.35 seconds. In the Funny Car final, he beat veteran Funny Car driver Ed "the Ace" McCulloch, with an elapsed time of 6.38 seconds and a speed of 229.69 miles per hour.

Funny Car Fact

Funny Cars came to be in 1964 when match racers found that if they moved the rear wheels forward it gave them more traction. Chrysler pioneered the Funny Car when in 1965, it built its altered-wheelbase Dodge and Plymouths. In 1966, the first fliptop Funny Car was introduced.

Left: Virtually all Funny Cars, even those with Ford or Chevrolet bodies, run the Hemi engine.

Below: Funny Cars have always provided more space for the sponsor's name than a dragster.

Chapter 7

Hemi Clone Cars

There was a time when the phrase "clone car" sent chills up the spine of any true automobile collector. The word "clone" was once a dirty word that meant rip-off. This was especially true when collectors were paying top dollar for certain models that looked like originals, but weren't. Recently, big-block Corvettes have been the hottest cars in the car collector world. To cash in on the demand, unscrupulous restorers take a small-block Corvette and magically transform it into a big block. The unsophisticated owner usually finds out years later after an expert has appraised the car.

Today, Hemi cars are commanding higher prices than Corvettes; but being duped by a Hemi clone has never been the problem it has been with other makes. The Hemi buyer generally possesses a higher level of knowledge that protects him from getting ripped off. More and more people, however, want the thrill of driving a Hemi without the astronomical cost

of an original. The solution is a clone or as they are called today, a "re-creation."

The first Hemi cars to be cloned were the rare 1964 and 1965 Super Stock Dodges and Plymouths. Chrysler only built a handful of these cars when they were new. Because they were race cars, they were treated carelessly with no thought of future value. Within a few years, most of these cars were sold and resold to other racers, with each successive owner adding more stress to the chassis and more

One of the most popular Mopars to clone is the 1965 A-990 Plymouth Super Stock race car.

modifications to the body. Today, an original 1964 or 1965 race car is very valuable and not the kind of car a collector would even drive to a mild-mannered cruise night. Clone car builders have stepped up to fill that need.

You could take a humble 1964 or 1965 Dodge or Plymouth two-door sedan and restore it to have the look and performance of a mid-1960s Super Stock. Certain visual cues were retained, such as the massive Hemi hood scoop, the fat rear tires, a tachometer on top of the instrument panel, and a slight nose-up stance. Because of the advances in engine technology, the Hemi engines they installed developed more power than the originals and could be driven on the street. This is the best of both worlds.

The popularity of the Hemi 'Cudas and Hemi Challenger R/Ts produced in 1970 and 1971 combined with their few numbers have made them a prime target for clone car builders. The depth of consumer knowledge on these cars, however, also makes it nearly impossible to pass off a clone as an original. Most builders simply fess up and admit the fact that the car is a clone.

Re-creating a Hemi 'Cuda is also easier today because of the number of reproduction parts available. A new Hemi engine can be bought directly from Mopar. And like the early Hemi race cars, one does not have to worry so much about damaging a rare original. Then owners of these reproduction vehicles have the freedom to drive them—and that's the most fun.

The law of supply and demand has caught up with Hemi cars. These exceptionally popular cars were built in low numbers and there are more people who want them than there are cars to go around. As their popularity continues to grow, there will be more clones built.

Monrovia, California's, Bob Mosher is the country's foremost restorer and builder of 1962 to 1965 Max Wedge and Hemi Mopars. Here are three of his recently completed 1965 models.

Having 500 horsepower on tap gives the owner the freedom to smoke the tires whenever he chooses.

In 1964, Chrysler only built a limited number of Hemi-powered Super Stock race cars. To get the most mileage from its investment, these cars were sold (given) directly to competitors. These cars were all built with special lightweight components. Like all other Mopars, these cars dominated the competition. And like most race cars, they were used and abused. Many were modified into altered-wheelbase racers and others were wrecked. Very few of the original 1964 cars remain. And those surviving cars are too valuable to drive on the street. The solution is to build a clone.

Hemi Clone Fact

Only one modification has to be made to the engine compartment of a 1964 or 1965 Plymouth or Dodge for a Hemi engine to fit. Because the engine is offset to the right, the right shock tower needs to be modified to clear the cylinder head.

Above: The Plymouth B-body cars built in 1964 were all constructed using Chrysler's superior unibody technology.

Left: Modern clone car builders strip the interiors of radios and heaters, in similar fashion to the original race cars.

Below: With available parts from Mopar, it's relatively easy to dress out a Hemi engine to look like the Hemis did in 1964.

One big advantage of having a clone of a former race car is that it can be built similar to the look of the original, with certain allowances made for modern technology. Mopar Super Stock springs are added to the rear and subframe connectors strengthen the body. In 1965, Chrysler only offered the 8 3/4 rear axle. Today, clone builders opt for the stronger Dana rear axle. And braking is improved with the addition of disc brakes.

Hemi Clone Fact

The cars that Dodge and Plymouth built in 1964 and 1965 had exceptionally large wheelwells. They adequately fit the 7-inch tires the sanctioning bodies required. With the exceptionally large tires available today, clone builders add mini-tubs to the rear by widening the rear wheelhouses by a couple inches.

The wide rear tires and RAW HEMI license plate are the only clues a librarian does not drive this sedate 1965 Plymouth sedan.

The Hemi engine in this 1965 Plymouth was created using a Mopar 440 block and adding Stage V Engineering's aluminum Hemi heads.

With a 10:1 compression Hemi engine, this race car clone can be easily driven on the street.

In 1965, Dodge and Plymouth both built a limited number of Super Stock cars with the code A-990. These cars were built using thinner-than-standard sheet metal for the body components. All of the cars Dodge and Plymouth built were two-door sedans, because they were the lightest body style. Plymouths were more popular for drag racing than Dodges, because of their shorter wheelbase and slightly lighter weight. But Dodge sponsored many competitors and their cars were competitive. This Coronet sedan pays homage to those racers.

Hemi Super Stock Parts Shopping Fact

The 1964 and 1965 Dodge and Plymouth Hemi Super Stock cars all used a cross-ram intake manifold. Because of the limited amount of these manifolds originally made, Mopar has stepped up to offer one for its Hemi crate engines. They also have the correct Holley carburetors.

Above: When Chrysler originally built its 1965 Super Stock cars they placed the battery in the trunk for improved traction. Clone car builders follow suit for originality, and placing it there also cleans up the engine compartment.

Left: The interior of all the A-990 race cars Chrysler produced was trimmed in tan vinyl. The tachometer on top of the instrument panel is where the racers placed it for a better view of engine rpms.

Below: The Hemi engine in this 1965 Dodge Coronet Super Stock clone is equipped with Stage V aluminum heads.

Advances in engine technology allow Super Stock clone car builders to be able to drive the streets on a regular basis. Something a real 1964 Hemi Super Stock could not do for long. The compression ratio on the clone car engines is in the pump-gas-friendly 10:1 area unlike the original 12.5:1 compression ratio. Today's clone builder is not restricted by a sanctioning body's rule structure to maintain certain aspects of the car stock. The goal of the clone car builder is to get the experience and have the look of the original Super Stock race cars.

Hemi Parts Shopping

Today, the Hemi clone builder has the vast resource of the Mopar parts catalog to rely upon. Mopar offers three street-friendly versions of the Hemi engine in crate form: a 426-ci with 465 horsepower, a 472-ci with 525 horsepower, and a 528-ci with 610 horsepower. In addition, Mopar offers bare blocks and cylinder heads for those who would prefer to build it themselves.

Left: Because the original 1964 Super Stock cars came from the factory with five-spoke American mags, most clone builders add them to their cars.

Right: The Mopar parts Hemi block in this 1964 Plymouth Super Stock clone has been bored and stroked to displace 510 cubic inches.

Left: The massive amount of torque provided by the Hemi engine can easily spin these P315-60R15 BFGoodrich drag radials.

If cars have souls, the soul of this 1970 Challenger could not be any happier. It started life with a six-cylinder engine under the hood and was originally purchased by an elderly woman. After 38,000 miles of easy driving, a pair of brothers, with a dream to build the ultimate Hemi Challenger street machine, purchased it. The Hemi engine that they installed came from a 1968 Plymouth Fury. The Fury's owner installed it years earlier because he pulled a heavy trailer and needed plenty of torque. The engine now displaces 520 cubic inches and develops 787 horsepower.

Challenger Fact

The total production of 1970 Challengers numbered 76,935. Of those, only 18,512 were R/T versions. That leaves 58,423 that can be modified with the addition of a Hemi engine. Lots of possibilities....

Left: Bright graphics accentuate the Challenger's exceptionally well-designed body. A small Challenger T/A spoiler has been added to the deck lid.

Right: Modifications have upped the horsepower on this Hemi engine to 787 horsepower.

Below: A Challenger T/A fiberglass hood and chin spoilers are easy upgrades for any Challenger.

In 1970, Dodge only built nine Challenger R/T convertibles with the Hemi engine. This would be the only year Dodge would build Challenger R/T convertibles. Today, it would cost at least a million dollars to buy an original 1970 Dodge Challenger R/T Hemi convertible. The next best thing is to find a low-mileage, highly optioned 1970 Challenger R/T convertible and install a Hemi engine. This particular Challenger R/T convertible started life with a 383 engine. The owner constructed this car to be exactly like a factory car. He makes no bones about the fact it's a clone and is actually proud that he could build one as good as the factory.

Hemi Challenger Fact

This car could easily fool an unknowing buyer. The owner left the original fender tag (because this car is highly optioned, there are two tags) in place, that when decoded will reveal that the car originally came with a 383 engine.

Above: Everything about this Hemi clone is accurate right down to the Shaker hood scoop.

Left: The big 426 Hemi in the engine compartment of this Challenger R/T clone looks as if it was there from day one.

Below: Challenger R/T convertibles are a rare find with any engine. Those with the Hemi are almost impossible to find.

This 1970 Challenger convertible started life as an ordinary Challenger. No high-performance options and no big engine. Its previous claim to fame was as a parts car for a high-dollar restoration of an R/T. The current owner saw it sitting in a corner of the restorer's shop and rescued it for a better life. He already had a highly modified Hemi engine and a vision to make an understated car that would have more bite than a pit bull at a postman's convention. Sharpening the teeth on that bite is a nitrous system. Enhancing the sinister look are wide steel wheels with dog dish hubcaps.

Hemi Clone Fact

E-body cars are getting harder and harder to find. Those R/T models with the original high-performance engines are out of reach for most enthusiasts. The key is finding an acceptable body, because all types of Mopar engines are available. Build it and drive it!

Left: The Hemi in this Challenger clone has been modified with a stroked crankshaft and nitrous.

Right: Interiors of clone cars can be tailored to suit the owner with aftermarket gauges and custom steering wheel.

Below: The small spoiler on the rear deck is from a Challenger T/A.

Nash Bridges was the only television show to prominently feature a muscle car—a Hemi 'Cuda. Well, almost. Don Johnson, who was the executive producer, desperately wanted a Hemi 'Cuda convertible, but once he found out the cost for a real one, he settled for a replica. The production company ended up building four 'Cudas that looked identical. Each was designed for a unique purpose, either close-ups, sound, jumps, or high-speed chase sequences. Not one of them had a Hemi engine and they were all quickly cobbled together. At the 2003 Barrett-Jackson auction, Don Johnson shilled the bid for one of these cars up to an amazing $148,500.

TV Car Fact

It may seem strange that there were four identical cars built for the filming of a television series. The fact is that it costs so much to produce a series like *Nash Bridges*, that if a day's lost because the star's car is being finicky, it would cost thousands of dollars in fixed costs and lost time that could not be recouped on the show's tight shooting schedule.

One component that was real on the *Nash Bridges* 'Cudas were the gilled front fenders.

From 30 feet you'd think you were looking at a real 1971 Hemi 'Cuda. Only one of the four was a real 'Cuda and only one was a 1971 model.

Each of the *Nash Bridges* cars was fitted with a fake Shaker hood scoop.

Chapter 8

CHALLENGER

DODGE

The New Hemi Cars & Trucks

By the end of the 1970s, no one would have predicted a third-generation Hemi engine, much less a revival of the muscle car era. In the 1970s, high-performance engines could never meet the emissions standards, much less the mileage requirements. But in 2003, Chrysler (now DaimlerChrysler) defied conventional logic and released the third-generation Hemi engine. First, they installed it in their Dodge Ram trucks and then in 2005 in the Chrysler 300C sedan and Dodge Magnum wagon. In doing so they re-created the modern American muscle car.

No one at DaimlerChrysler stood up and shouted, "Let's build another Hemi engine!" It all happened as part of the development of a new V-8 engine to replace Chrysler's aging 5.9-liter V-8. In 1997, work started on what would be a new truck engine. The engine group's goal was to produce a new V-8 that was elegantly simple. They looked at many engine designs in the process, including 30 different valvetrain arrangements. They settled on a 5.7-liter Hemi design because it met all of their requirements for simplicity, durability, and horsepower.

While the new 5.7 Hemi was in its later stages of development, DaimlerChrysler engineers were working on a new car to replace

When introduced in 2005, the new Dodge Magnum offered the same new Hemi engine as the Chrysler 300C along with the versatility of a station wagon. *David Newhardt*

its aging LH front-wheel-drive car line. This new car would have striking new proportions because it would be a rear-wheel drive. As soon as the product planners found out about the new Hemi V-8, it was added to the list of engines that would be available. Dubbed LX, this new platform was the basis for the 2005 Chrysler 300C and Dodge Magnum. For 2006, Dodge added a new Charger built on the LX platform. With 345 horsepower, the new Hemi engine provided outstanding performance for these exciting new models.

Within the DaimlerChrysler organization is a small group of engineers known as SRT (Street and Racing Technology). SRT engineers own the big hypodermic needle that injects the steroids into its base products to turn them into super cars. It hadn't been long after the first 5.7-liter-powered Hemi rolled off the assembly line that the group met to decide what kind of magic it would work on this new engine in the LX platform.

The new Hemi-powered 2006 Dodge Ram 1500 TRX4 Off-Road model features 17-inch aluminum wheels, aggressive off-road tires, skid plates, and a limited-slip differential. Fog lamps and "TRX4 Off-Road" decals accentuate the exterior of this attractive pickup.

For the 2006 model year they released SRT8 versions of the Dodge Charger, Chrysler 300C, and the Dodge Magnum. The heart of this exciting package is the new Hemi engine with an increased displacement to 6.1 liters, a higher compression ratio, and a new camshaft. The end result is a horsepower rating of 425. Added to the package is a special suspension package and wide Goodyear tires on 20-inch wheels. Any one of these SRT8 cars is capable of going from 0 to 60 miles per hour in 5 seconds.

At the 2006 Detroit Auto Show, Dodge introduced its Hemi-powered Challenger concept car. Dodge designers drew heavily on the 1970 Challenger in designing the new one. In doing so they captured the essence of the original Challenger with its signature lines, aggressive air-grabbing grille, and bold colors and graphics. DaimlerChrysler will not confirm that this latest Challenger will be built, but save your money just in case.

With Chrysler's Multi-Displacement System (MDS), its new Hemi V-8 engine transitions from eight cylinders to four in 40 milliseconds (0.040 seconds). This improves fuel economy without a change in driver experience. *David Newhardt*

David Newhardt

When Chrysler's engineers started to work on its new LX rear-wheel-drive platform, they all agreed that there would be no compromises. Much to their delight was the release of the new 5.7-liter Hemi engine that would find a home in the new Chrysler 300C and Dodge Magnum. The 300's long hood and tall sedan styling give it an unmistakably strong presence. Its high beltline and dramatic design makes every other luxury sedan on the road look boring. The package Chrysler's engineers created is stylish, and with the new Hemi, fun to drive.

New Hemi Fact

The MDS system on the new Chrysler 300C's Hemi engine deactivates four of the engine's eight cylinders when the power requirement lessens. This innovative system allowed Chrysler to release this car without a gas-guzzler penalty because of the high mileage that can be attained. When needed, the four deactivated cylinders seamlessly spring into action.

The grille of the new 300 makes a strong statement that this *is* the new face of Chrysler. *David Newhardt*

Chrysler's Electronic Stability Program (ESP) allows the driver to push the car aggressively before it engages. This system helps the driver maintain directional stability on all types of driving surfaces. *David Newhardt*

The new 300C's 120-inch wheelbase and "wheels to the corners" design provide a more balanced ride and increases interior space. *David Newhardt*

David Newhardt

When Chrysler designed its new LX platform, in addition to the new 300C, they also created a station wagon for Dodge, named Magnum. The new Dodge Magnum delivers the benefits of a sport utility vehicle with the comfort of a passenger car and the performance of a 1960s-era muscle car. The Chrysler LX designers once again veered off the straight and narrow path to offer a new twist on an old design. The large cargo opening is accessed through a rear tailgate door that is hinged midway between the C- and D-pillars. This brilliant, but simple, design solution gives unprecedented access to the rear cargo area because of the large opening created by the uniquely hinged rear door.

5.7-Liter Hemi Specs

Displacement: 345 cubic inches

Bore: 3.92 inches

Stroke: 3.58 inches

Compression ratio: 9.6:1

Horsepower: 340 @ 5400 rpm

Torque: 390 ft-lb @ 4000 rpm

Above: Dodge designers created a special engine cover for the Magnum's Hemi V-8. *David Newhardt*

Right: The Magnum's comfortable leather seats and well-laid-out instrument panel make driving the Magnum effortless. *David Newhardt*

The low roofline of the new Dodge Magnum gives it unique proportions, unlike any other station wagon. *David Newhardt*

In 1970, Chrysler, in conjunction with Hurst, released a special gold and white edition of the Chrysler 300C, the 300-Hurst (also known as the 300-H). Chrysler obviously wanted to cash in on the muscle car mania that was sweeping the nation, and what better name in the performance industry to team up with than Hurst? History has repeated itself with Performance West's new Hurst Edition of Chrysler's 300. The House of Kolor Pearl white and gold provides a perfect accent for the Chrysler's latest version of the 300. Accenting the striking paint job is a set of Oasis 22x9-inch alloy wheels that mount Toyo 285/35R22 Proxes S/T tires. A Kenne Bell engine management system allows the Hurst 300's Hemi to freely spin these large tires.

Hurst Edition 300 Features

Cat back exhaust: Magnaflow

Upgraded brakes and rotors: Stainless Steel Brake Co.

Custom leather interior: Katzkin leather in white and gold

Hurst monogrammed floor mats: Custom Mat

Custom audio system: Boston Acoustics

Above: The Chrysler 300 Hurst Edition rides with a 1½-inch lower stance due to a special set of springs.

Right: For a cleaner custom look, the vertical bars have been removed from the Hurst 300's grille.

Left: Special Hurst Edition emblems have been added to the front fenders of the this custom Chrysler 300.

Shortly after the introduction of the new Chrysler 300C and Dodge Magnum, there were rumors of a new Dodge Charger based on the LX platform. Dodge's product planners were smart enough to realize that the excellent LX platform, along with the new Hemi engine wrapped in a new Charger body, would be a winner—and they were right. When the crew in Chrysler's Street and Racing Technology group saw the new Charger, they were wired. They quickly set out to create exactly what performance enthusiasts want in their modern American muscle car: more power, world-class ride and handling, outstanding braking, aggressive-looking exterior upgrades, and a race-inspired interior. And that's exactly what they created in the all-new 2006 Dodge Charger SRT8.

SRT8 6.1-Liter Hemi Specs
Displacement: 370 cubic inches
Bore: 4.06 inches
Stroke: 3.58 inches
Compression ratio: 10.3:1
Horsepower: 425 @ 6200 rpm
Torque: 420 ft-lb @ 4800 rpm

Left: All SRT8 Chargers have a special hood with a scoop that channels cool air to the engine compartment.

Right: The SRT8 Charger is fitted with SRT-developed five-spoke 20-inch forged aluminum wheels. The tires are high-performance Goodyear Supercar F1 three-season tires with asymmetrical tread.

Below: The Charger SRT8's rear fascia features integrated lower strakes to direct airflow and a pair of cutouts that accommodate the twin 3.5-inch exhaust tips.

Larry Weiner's Performance West Group has been building image cars and trucks for Chrysler for several years. Weiner has an excellent knowledge of automotive history and a finely tuned sense of the latest automotive trends before they appear on the horizon. When Dodge released the new Hemi engine in the 2003 Ram truck, his synapses fired and he came up with the Rumble Bee concept. Dodge executives liked the Rumble Bee concept so well that they turned it into a production vehicle. In the Spring of 2004 the first Rumble Bees were shipped to dealers. Dodge offered the Rumble Bee in two colors: Black or Solar Yellow with contrasting bumblebee stripes across the rear of the bed with the Rumble Bee logo. In addition to the standard 345-horsepower Hemi engine, Dodge added a body-color hood scoop, brushed aluminum fuel filler door, body-color taillight guards, and chrome exhaust tip.

Rumble Bee Specs

Paint: SpectraFlair Holographic Metalflake B-5 Blue

Supercharger: Kenne Bell Performance Products "Blowzilla"

Wheels: Oasis Alloy M1 24-inch diameter x 10 inches wide

Tires: BFGoodrich 305/35ZR24

Interior: Katzkin Custom Leather and Suede

Added to the Performance West Rumble Bee prototype is a special Rumble Bee logo similar to the original Super Bee logo used in the 1960s.

Just barely visible between the wheel spokes is the stainless steel brakes' red Force 10 caliper.

Under the Rumble Bee's scooped hood is a Kenne Bell supercharged Hemi that develops an estimated 500 horsepower.

With a vehicle as interesting and versatile as the new Dodge Magnum, it was difficult for Chrysler's team of SRT engineers to stay away. Especially since the technology for the SRT8 engine and chassis upgrades had already been engineered for the Chrysler 300 and Dodge Charger. Up front, Dodge designers added a new front fascia that helps brake cooling through a pair of integrated ducts. They also added a unique body-color grille insert with chrome trim, satin-finish front and rear bumper inserts, body-color mirrors and door handles, and SRT badging. Dodge is limiting the SRT8 Magnum to three exterior colors: Silver, Black, and Inferno Red.

SRT8 Specs

0 to 60: 5.24 seconds

Quarter-mile: 13.66 seconds @ 105.4 miles per hour

Top Speed: 172 miles per hour (chip limited)

Braking, 60 miles per hour to 0: 118 feet
Base price: $37,320

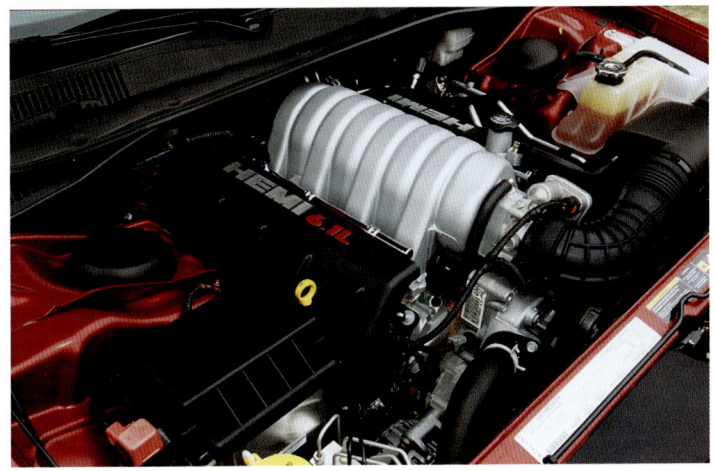

Left: Although almost completely hidden by the special intake manifold and engine covers, the Magnum SRT8's 425-horsepower Hemi engine is painted Hemi Orange.

Right: The Dodge Magnum SRT8's interior features power-adjustable, highly bolstered sport seats trimmed in suede and leather. Dodge also added "carbon fiber" leather trim on the steering wheel, and special carbon fiber finishing on the center stack.

Below: All four wheels of the Magnum SRT8 feature performance four-piston brake calipers by Brembo. In addition, the SRT8 has 360x32mm vented rotors up front, with 350x26mm vented rotors in the rear.

Photo Courtesy of DaimlerChrysler

At the 2006 Detroit International Auto Show, Dodge unveiled its 2006 Challenger concept car. The designers at Chrysler's West Coast Pacifica studios drew on the original Challenger's classic lines to create this modern American muscle car. They knew that a muscle car, any muscle car, has to have certain key attributes: signature lines, lots of horsepower, an aggressive grille, bold wheels and tires, and stunning colors and graphics. This hot-looking coupe is built on a modified version of the LX platform that's used on the Charger and the Magnum. Under the hood is a 425-horsepower 6.1-liter Hemi engine backed by a six-speed manual transmission. Dodge will not say if this car will go into production. But, save your money just in case.

Muscle Car Fact

In the ongoing poker game between American and foreign automakers to develop new models, the American manufacturers have a pair of aces up their collective sleeves. It's the muscle car. By drawing heavily on their iconic cars of the past, the American companies will have a car that cannot be copied. Ford proved this with the 2005 Mustang and now Dodge, and is in a position to do the same with the Challenger.

Right: The Hemi engine Dodge engineers installed in the Challenger concept is the same 6.1-liter, 425-horsepower version that's installed in SRT8 Chargers. *Photo Courtesy of DaimlerChrysler*

Left: With its Tuff-style wheel and Pistol Grip shifter, the interior of the Challenger concept has the same bold references to the classic 1970 Challenger as the exterior. *Photo Courtesy of DaimlerChrysler*

Right: The rear of the Challenger concept features flush bumpers with a pair of rectangular exhaust tips extending from the bottom edge. *Photo Courtesy of DaimlerChrysler*

INDEX